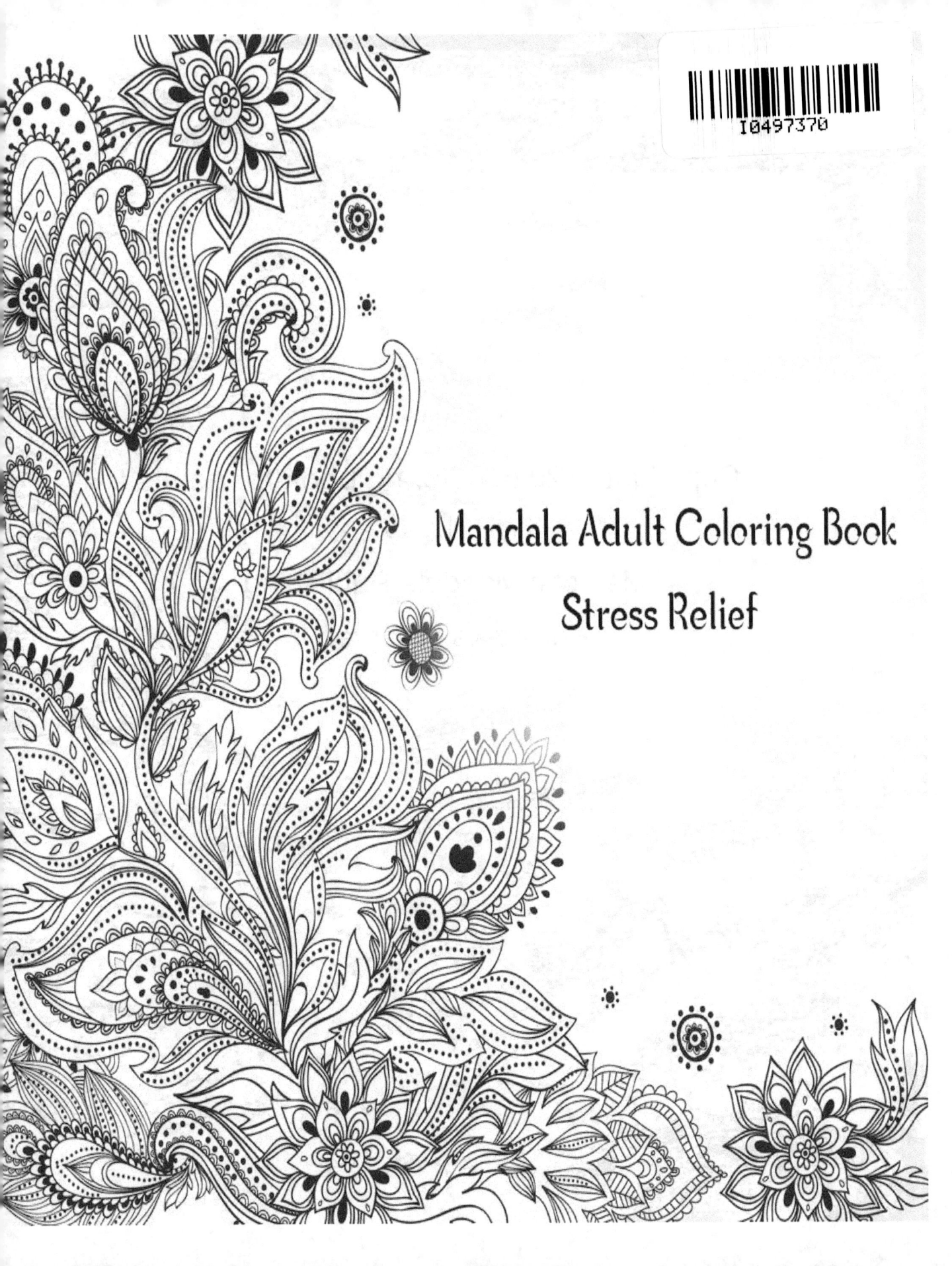

Mandala Adult Coloring Book
Stress Relief

Copyright © 2020, coloring book for adults

by

Majestic Mandala Publishing

all rights reserved.

This Book Belongs To

....

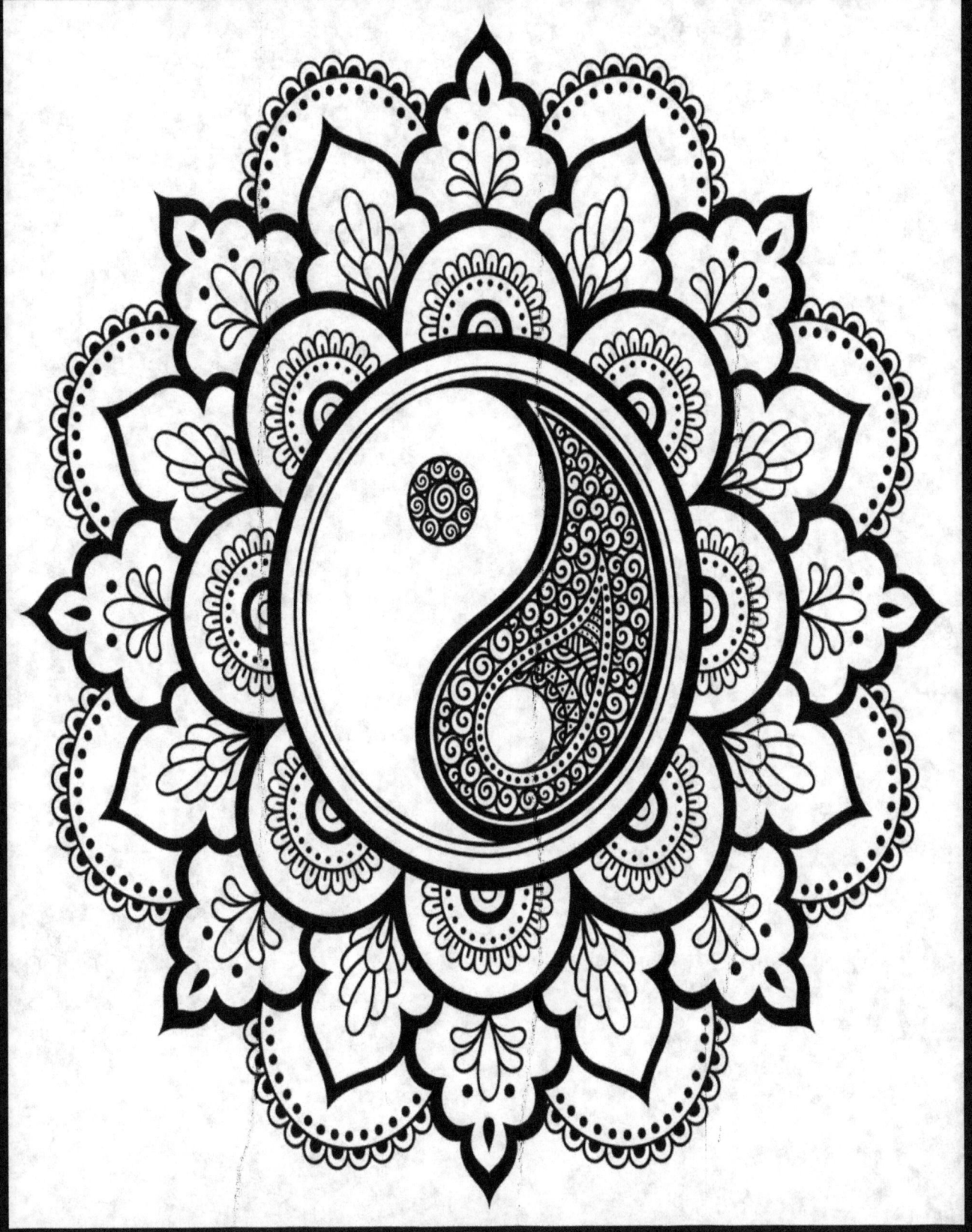

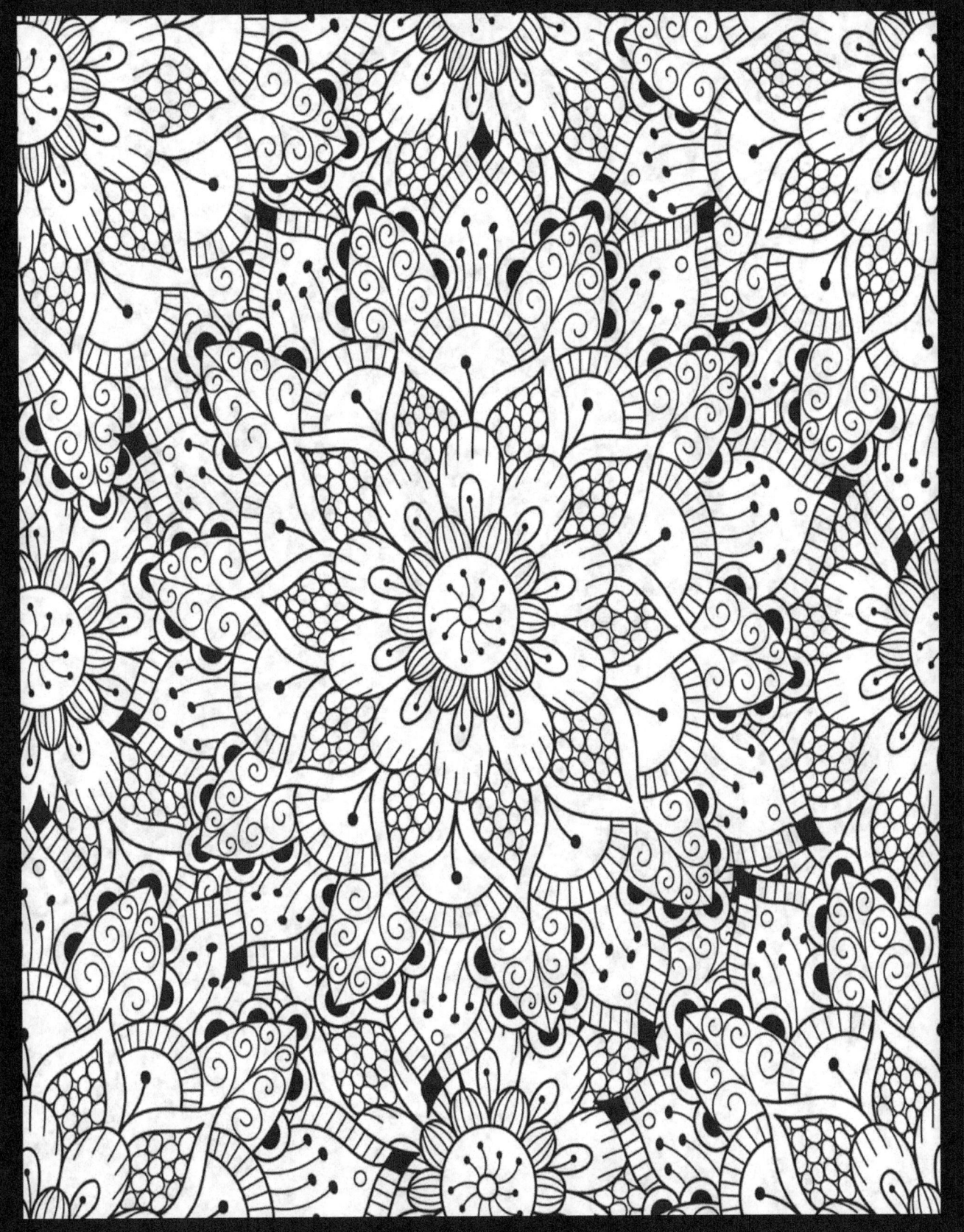

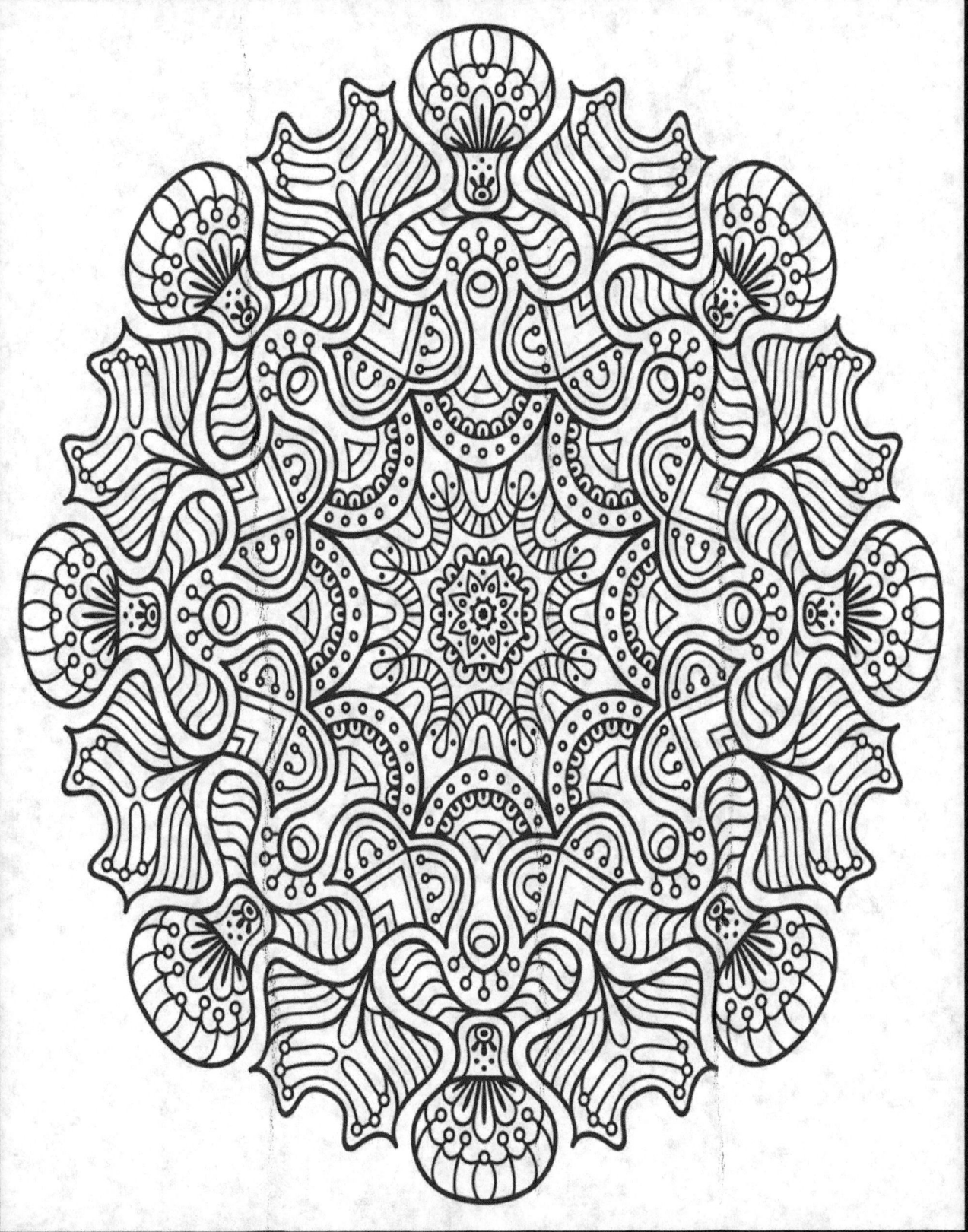

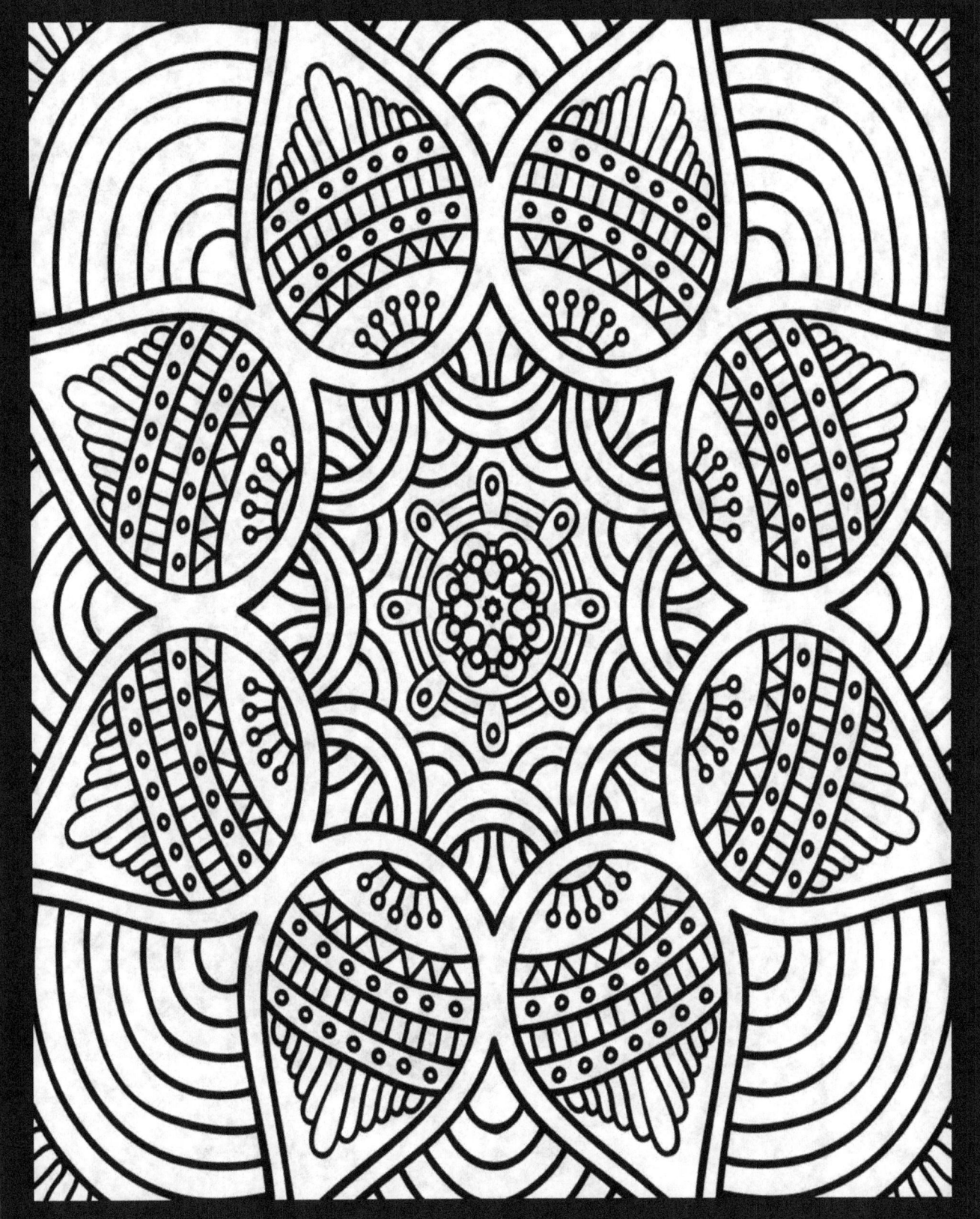

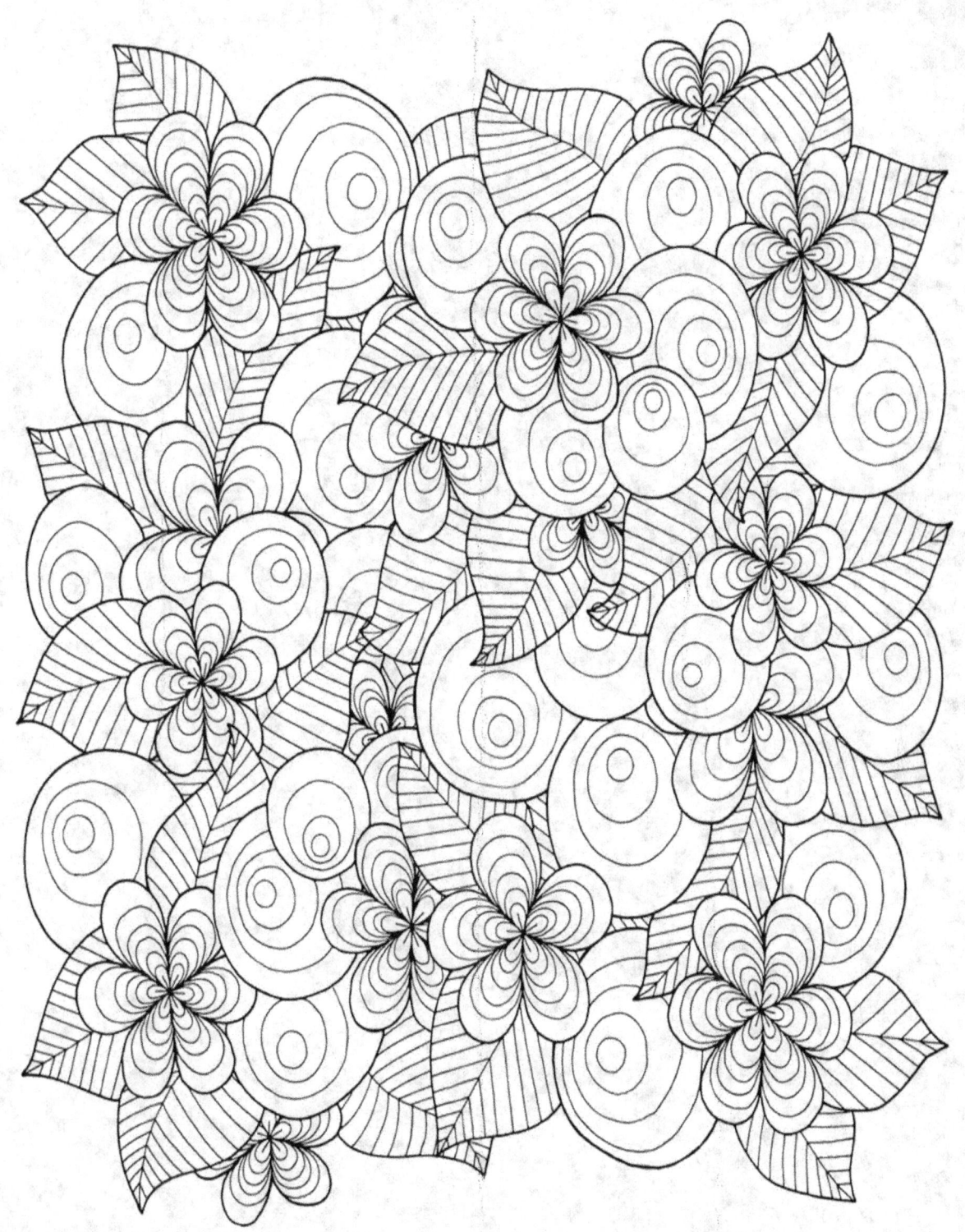

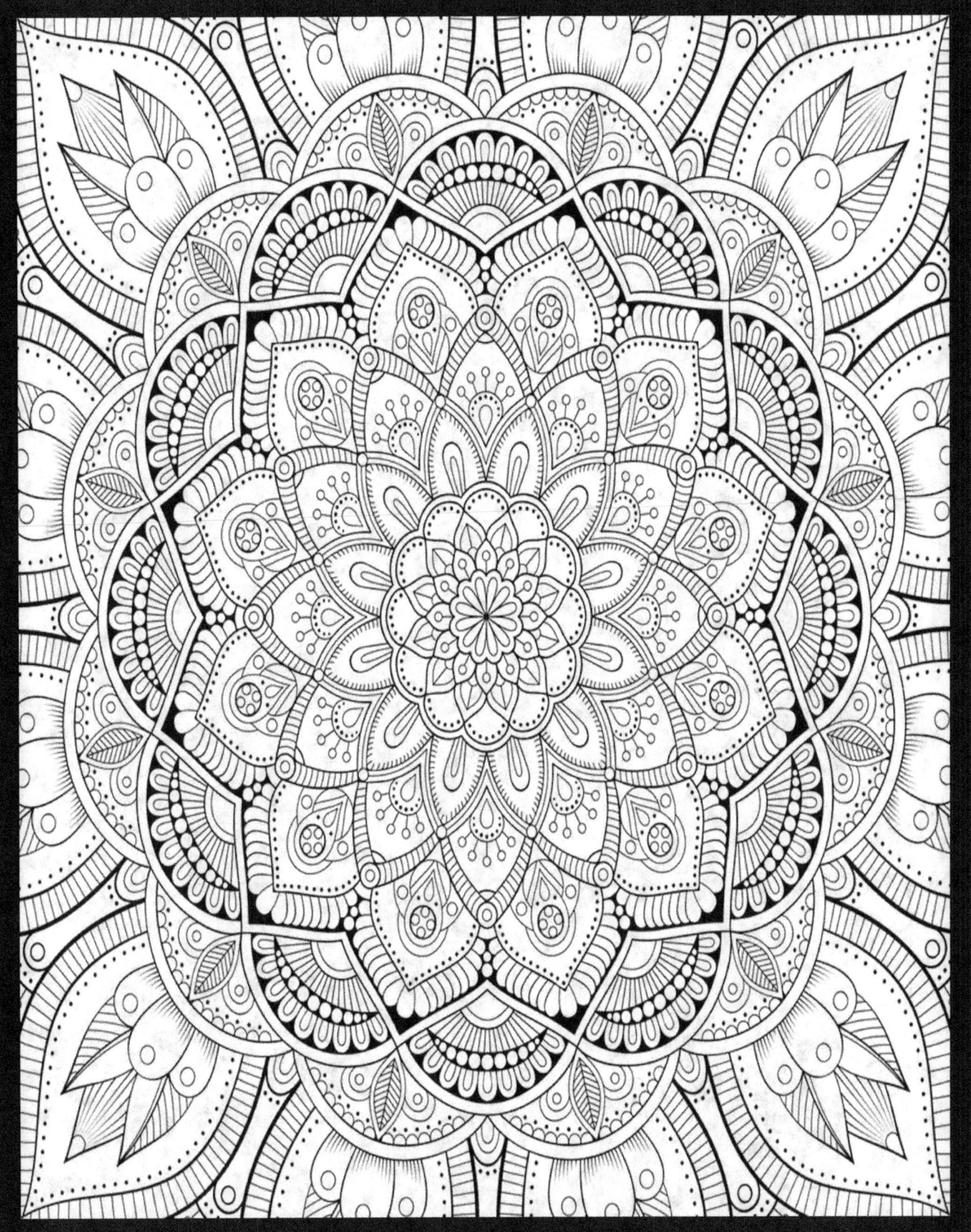

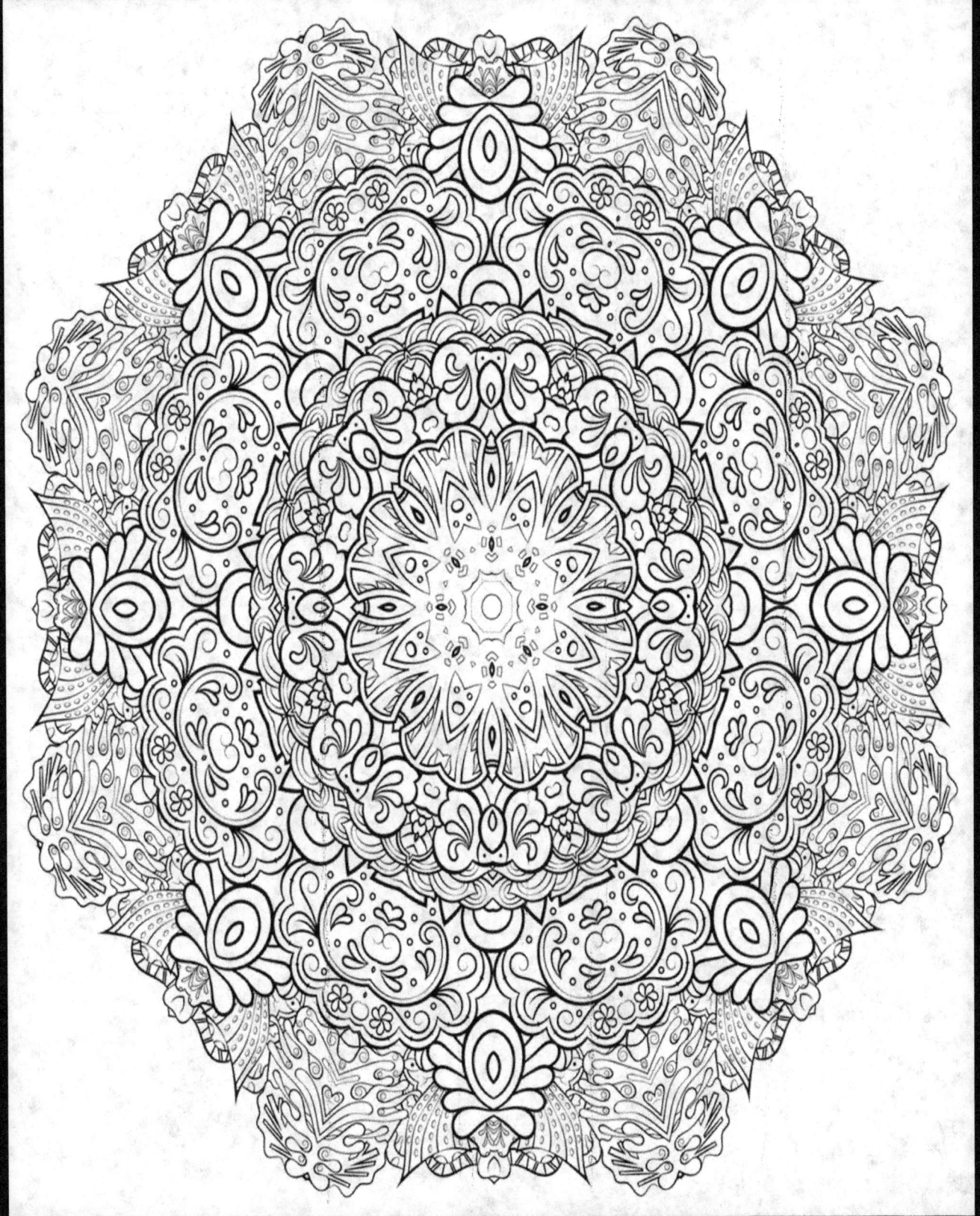

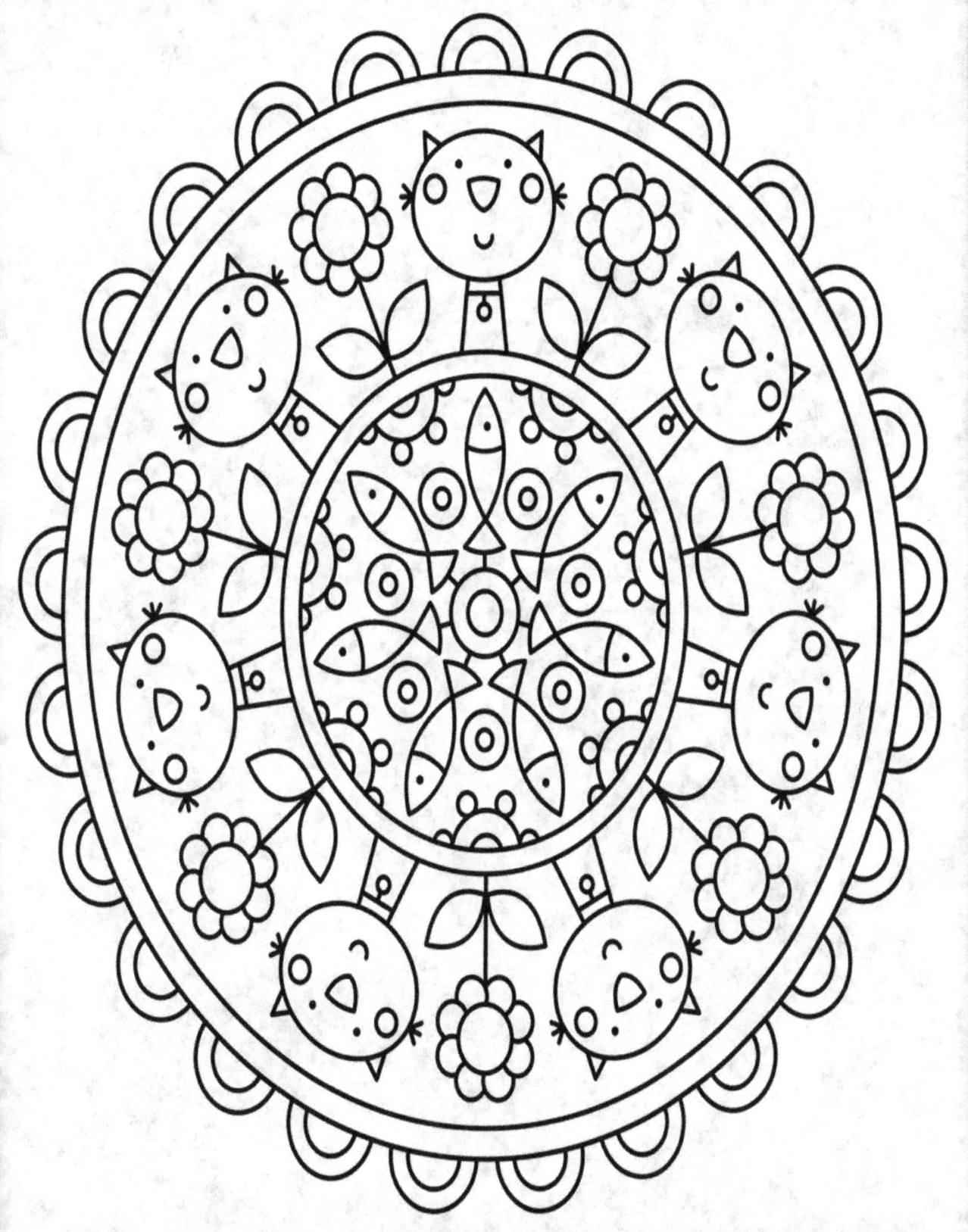

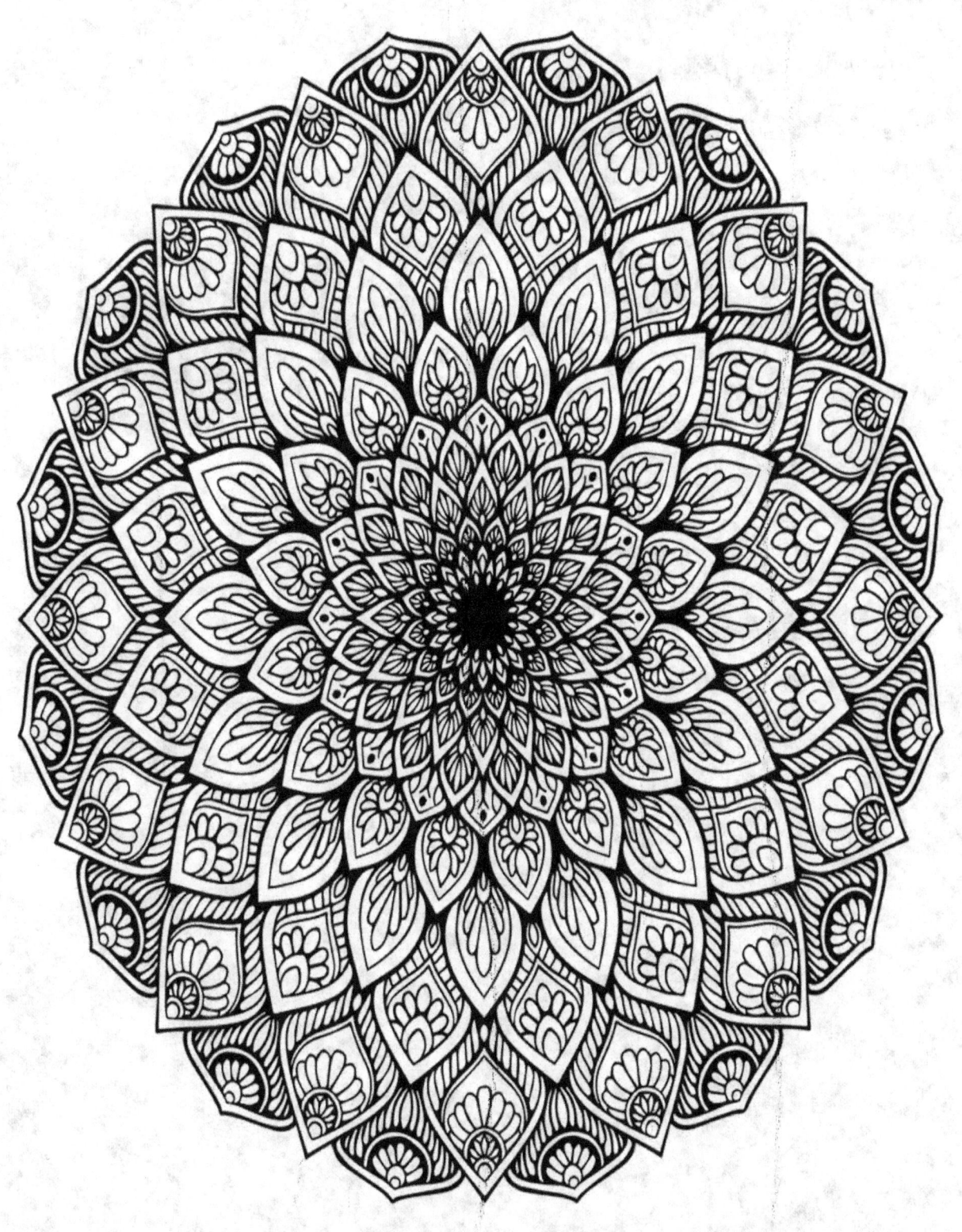

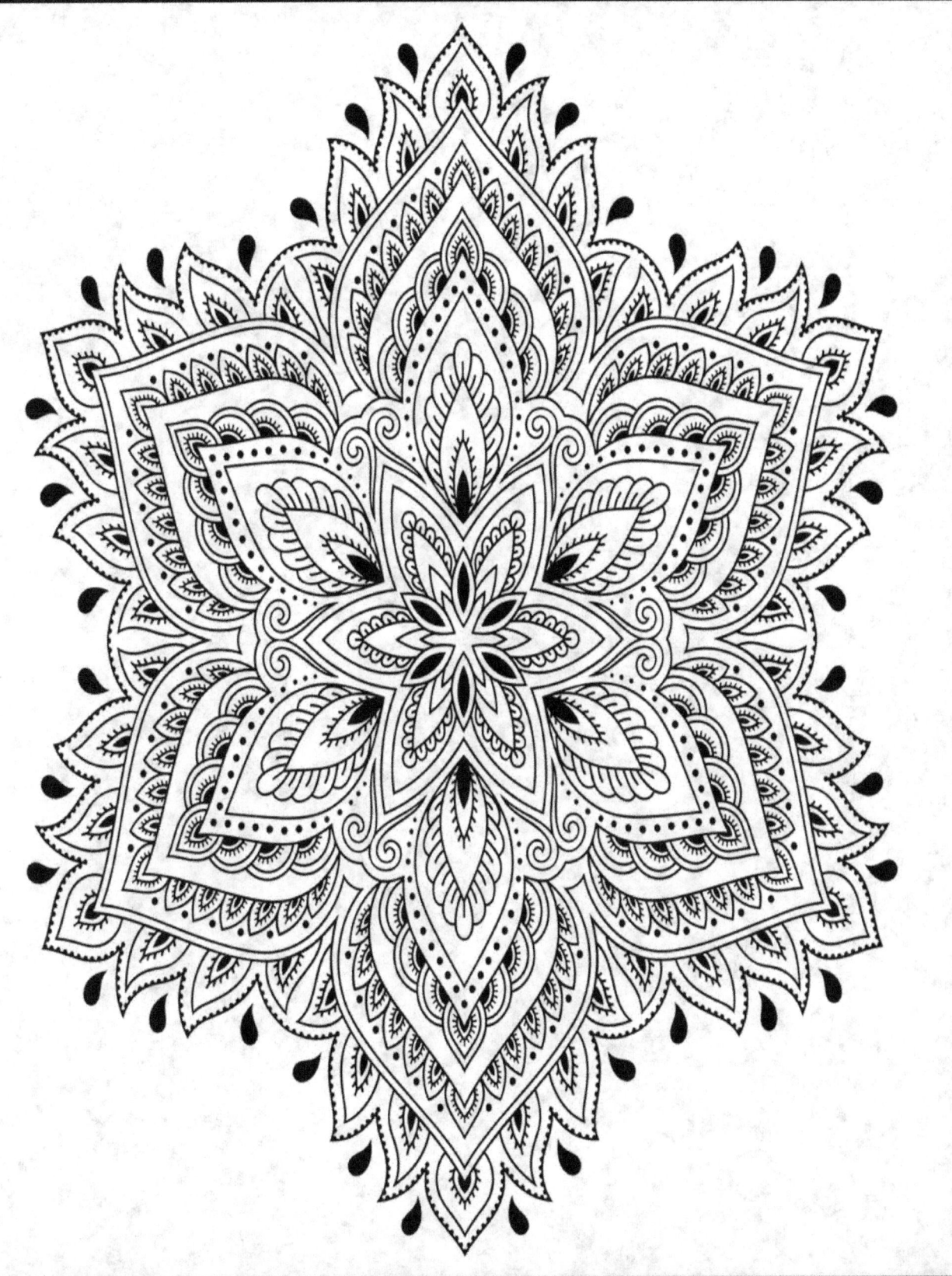

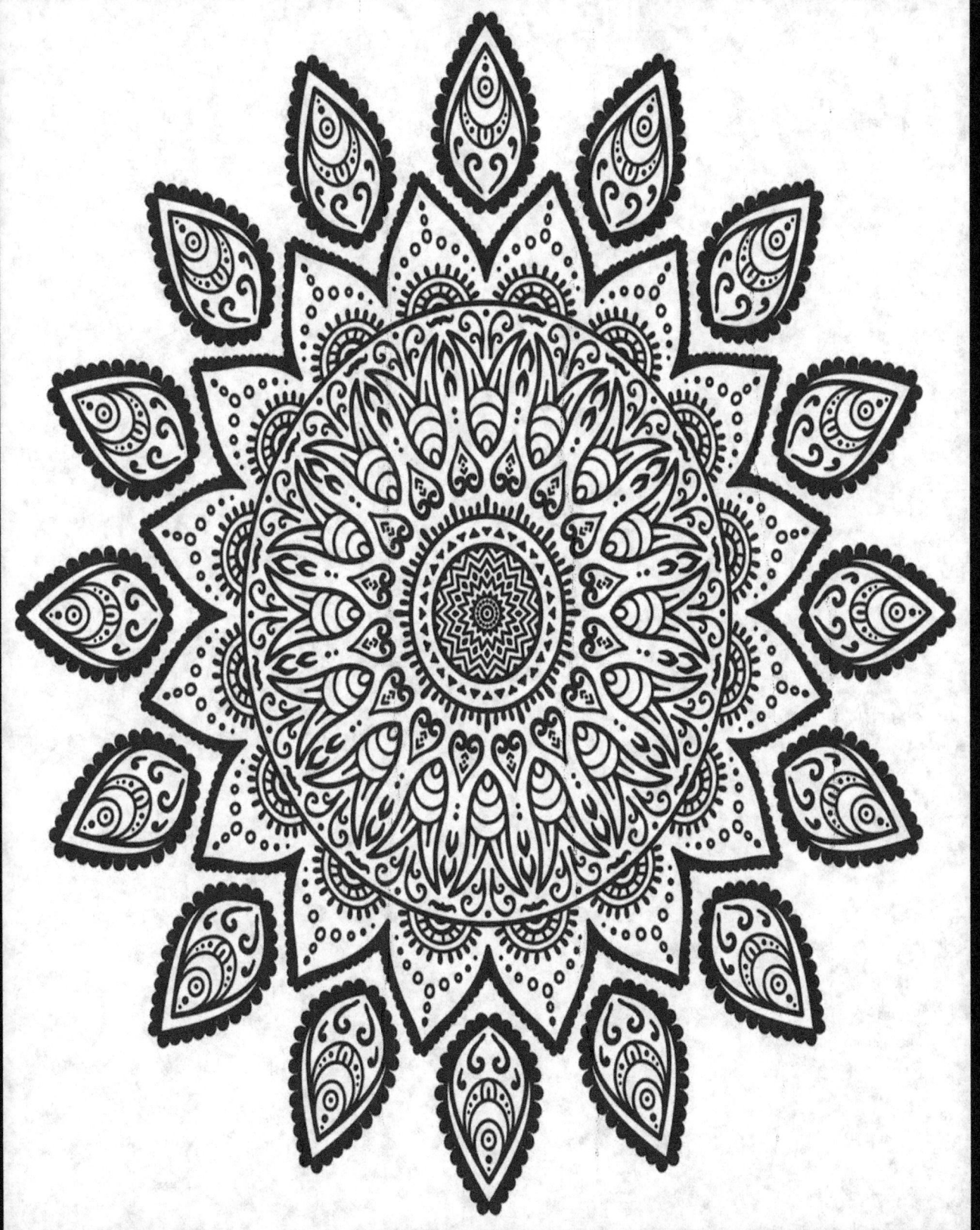

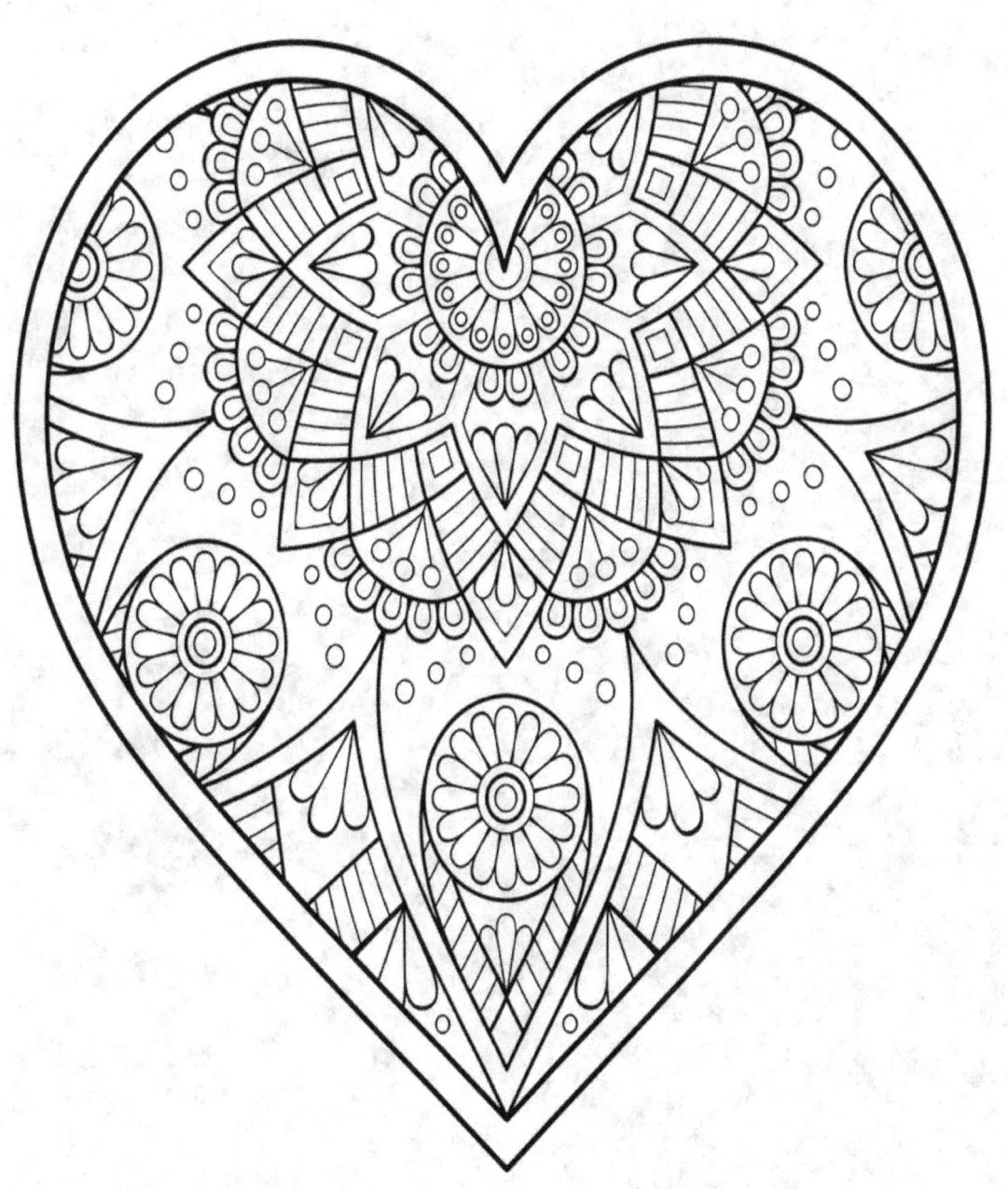

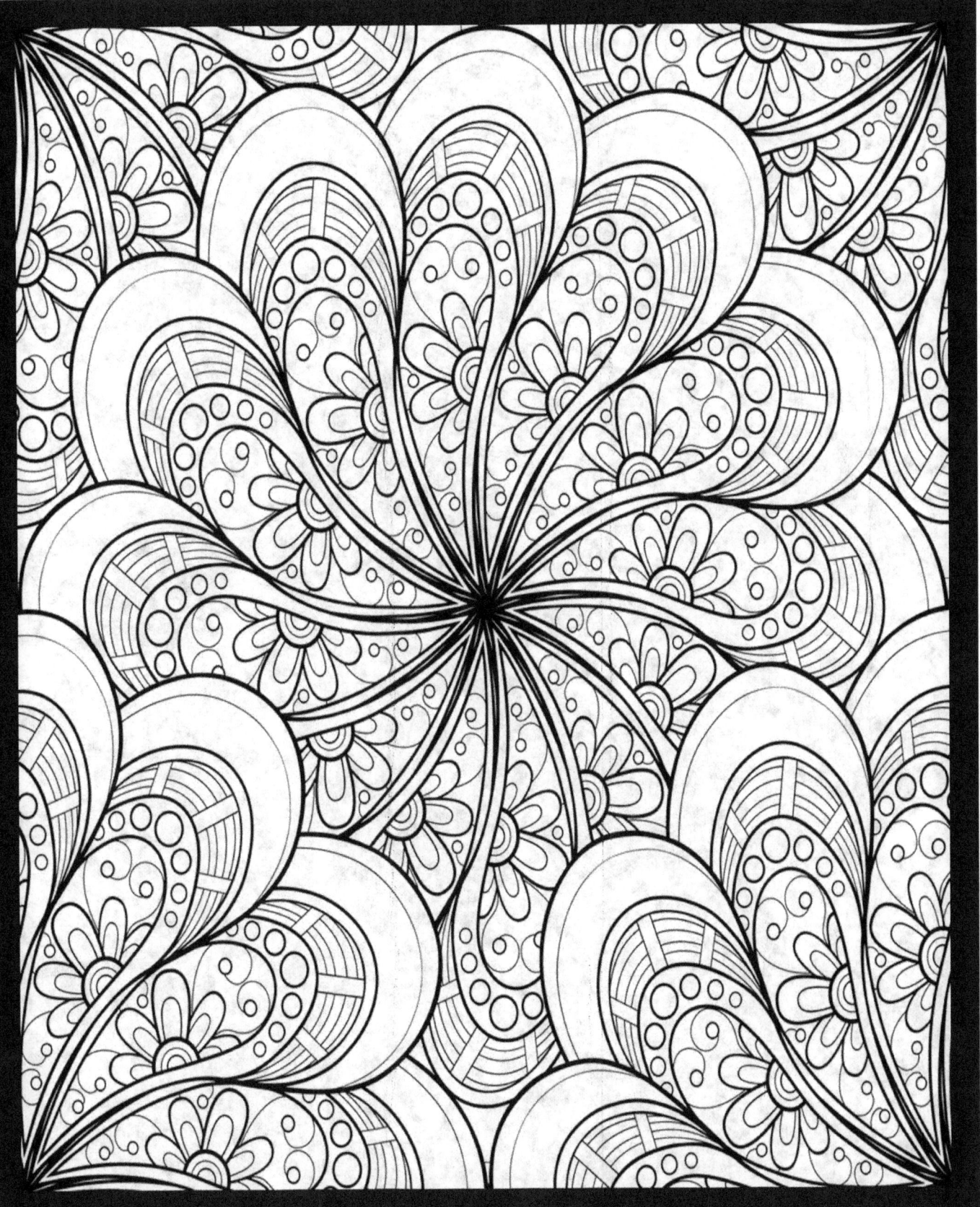

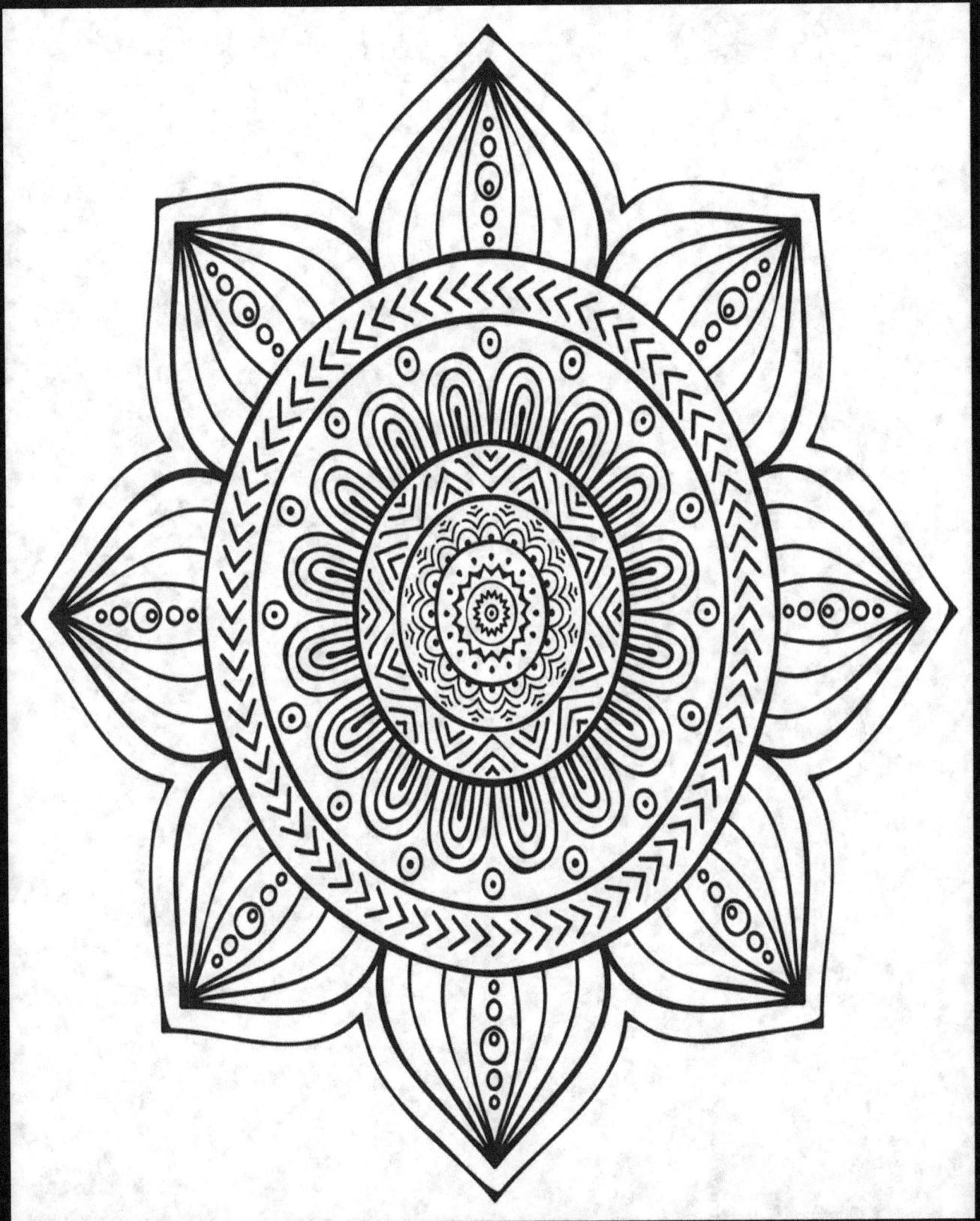

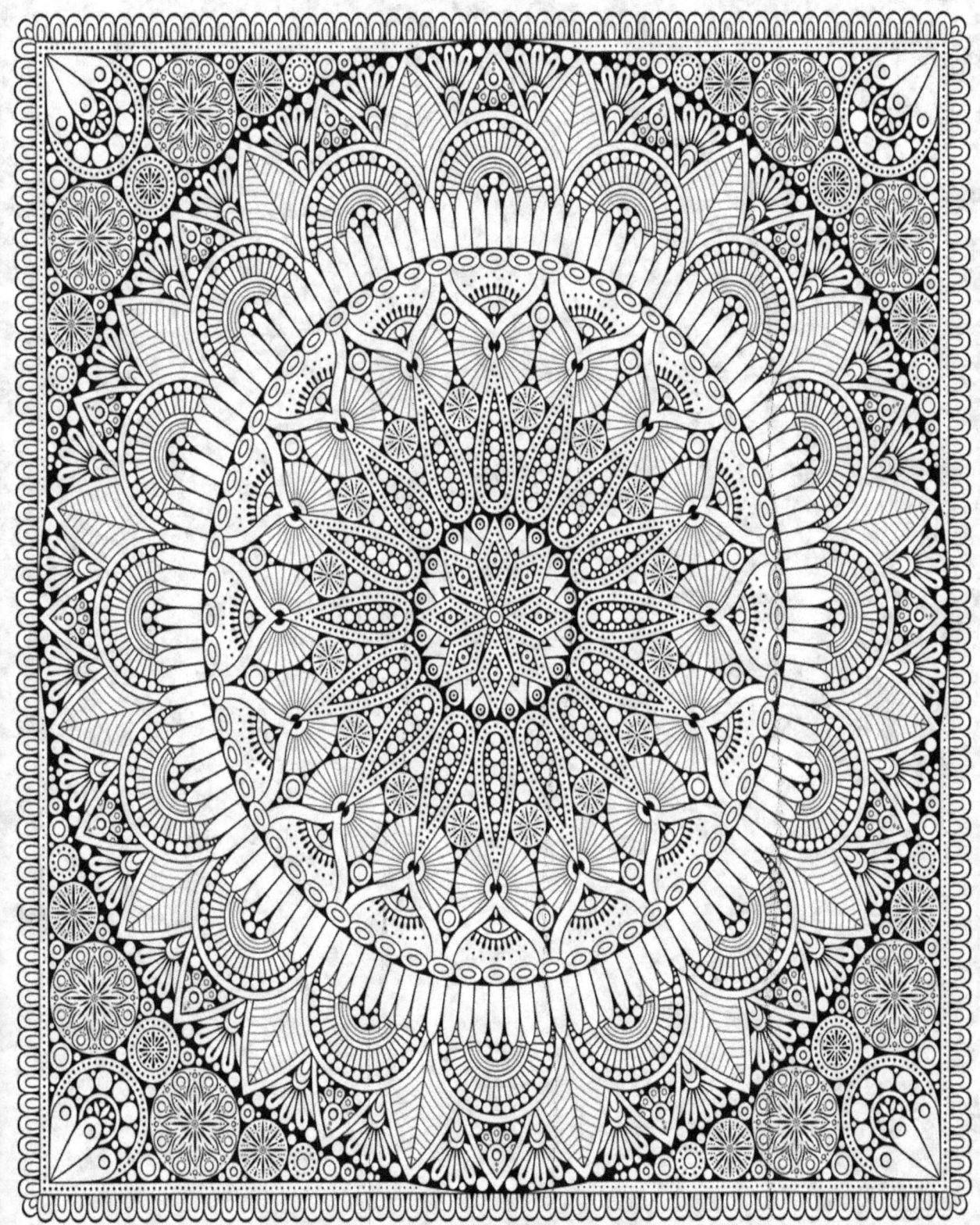

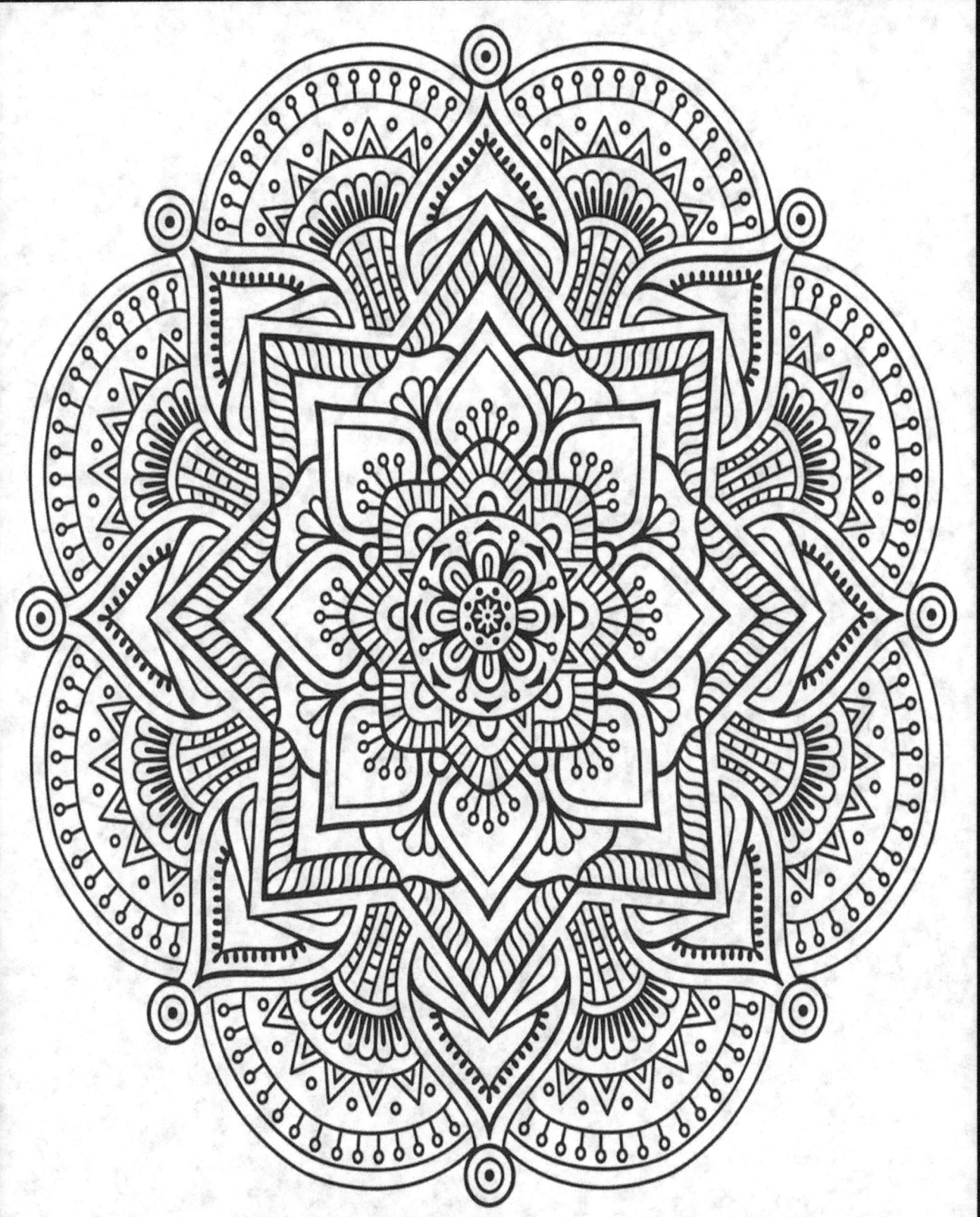

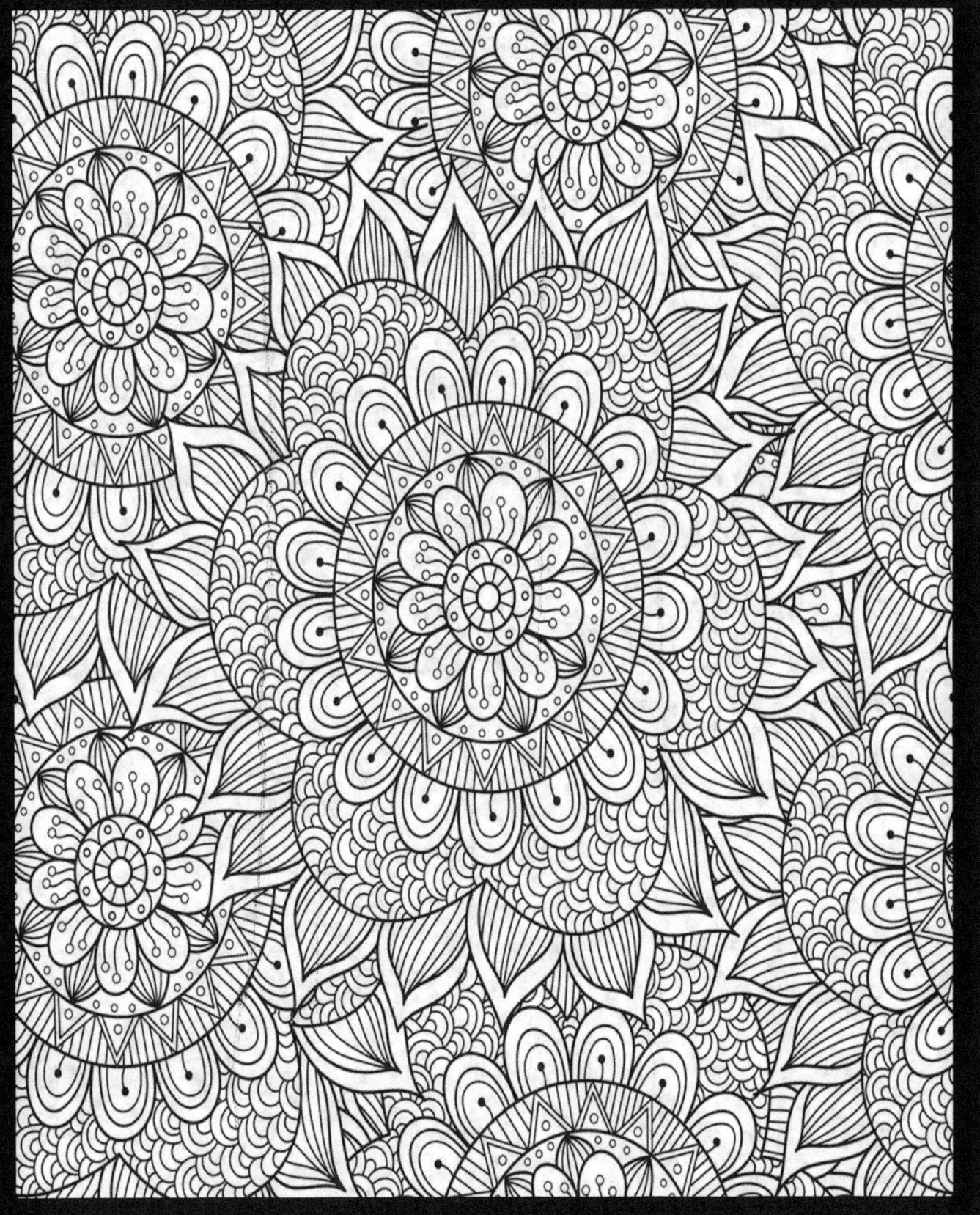

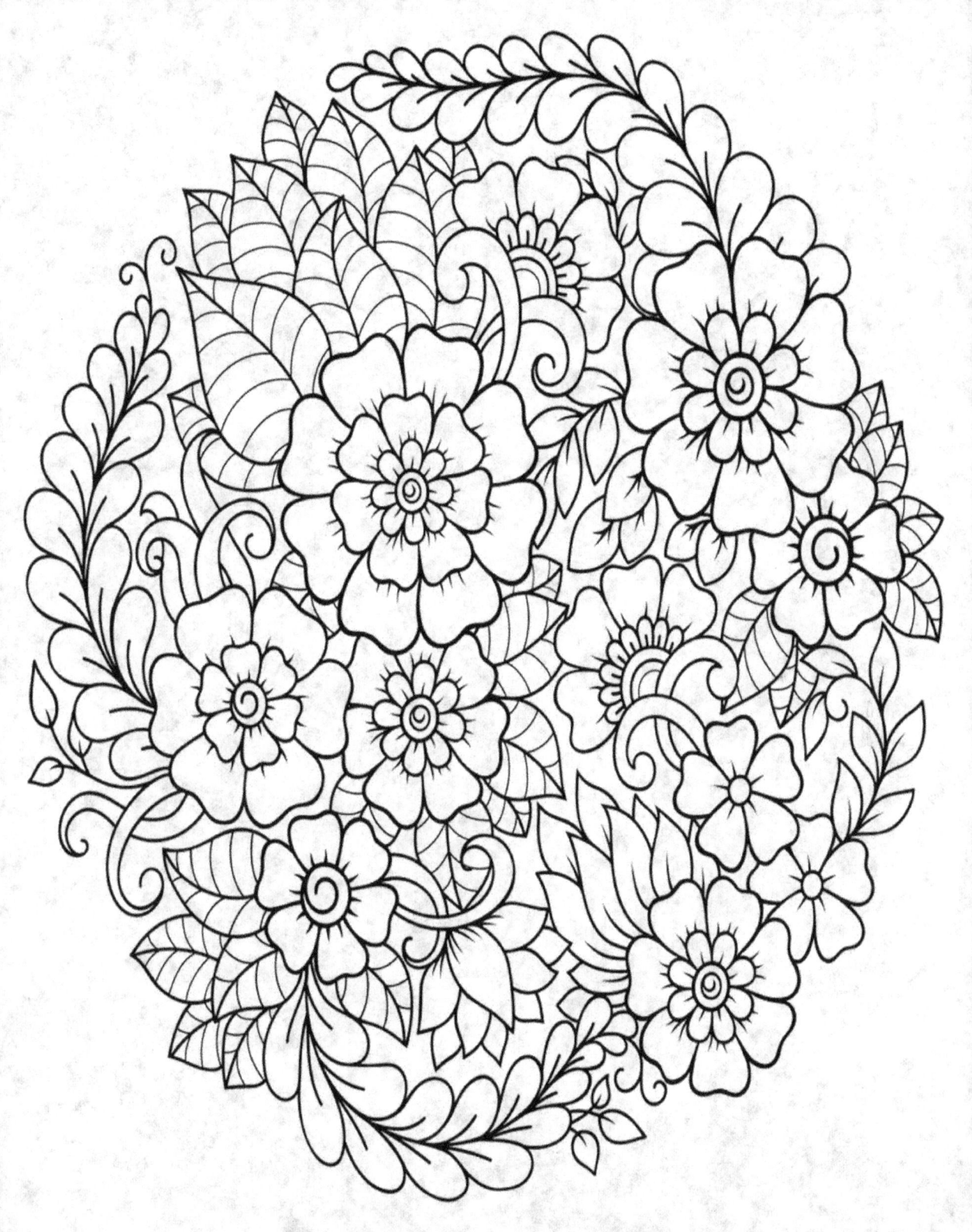

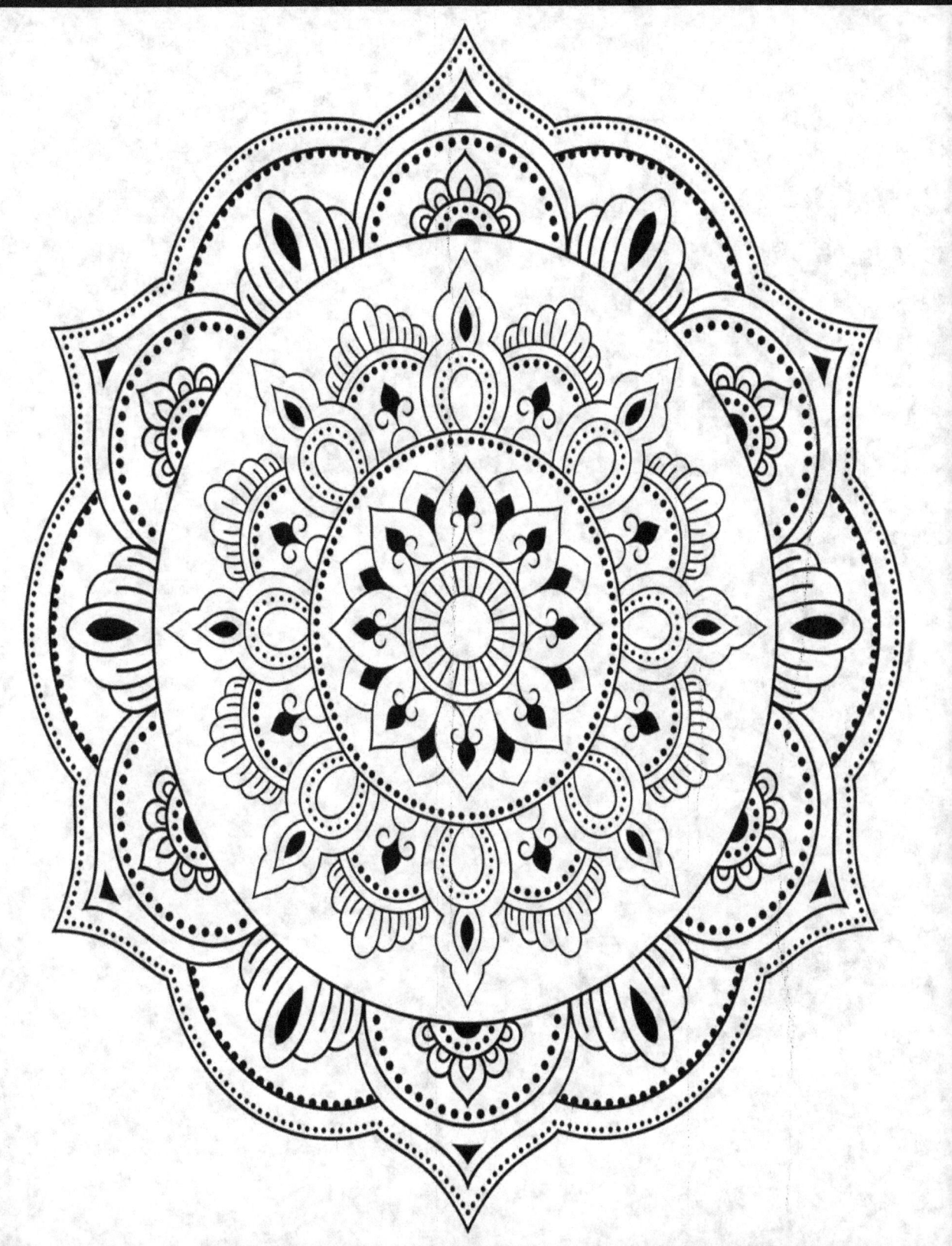

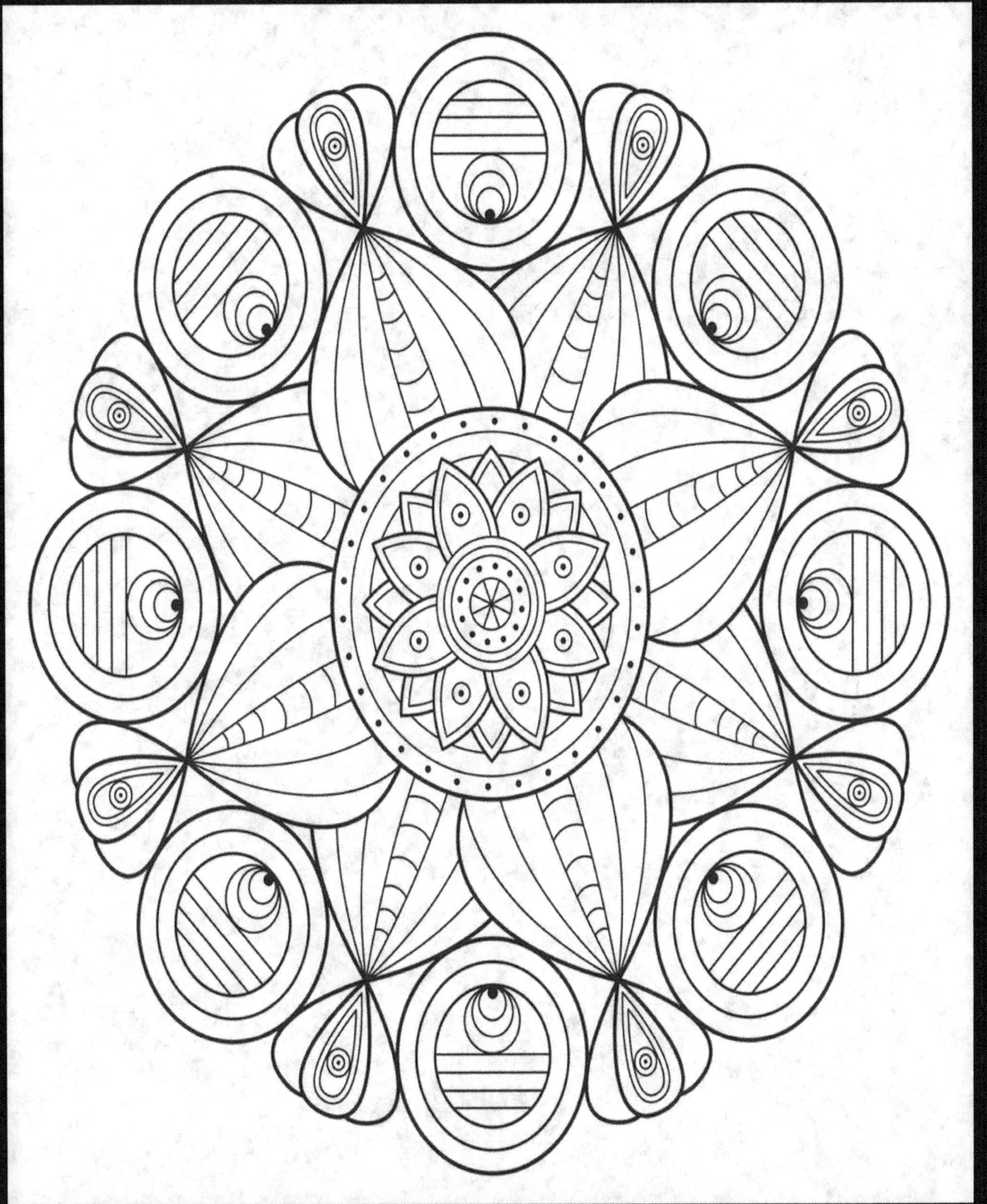

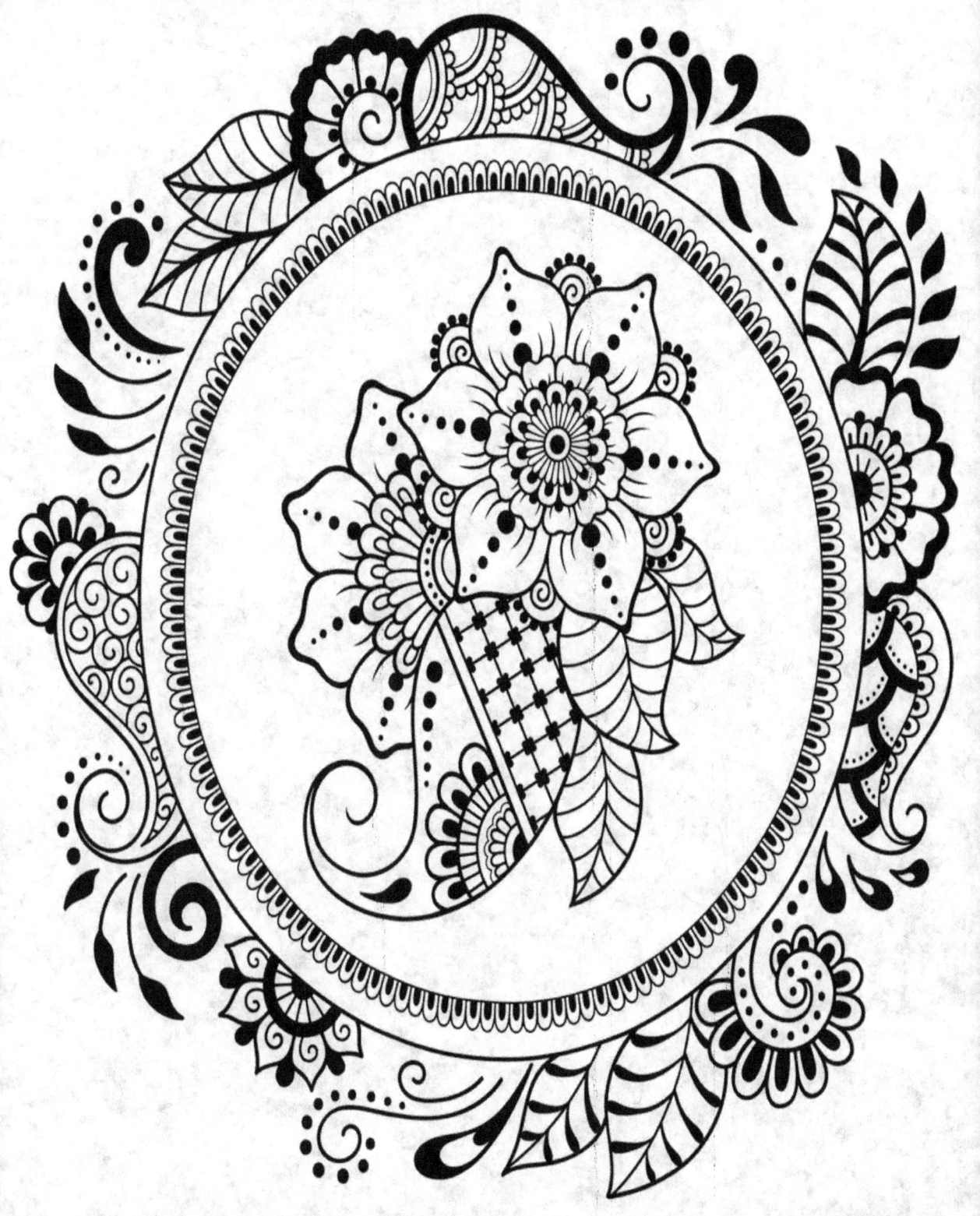

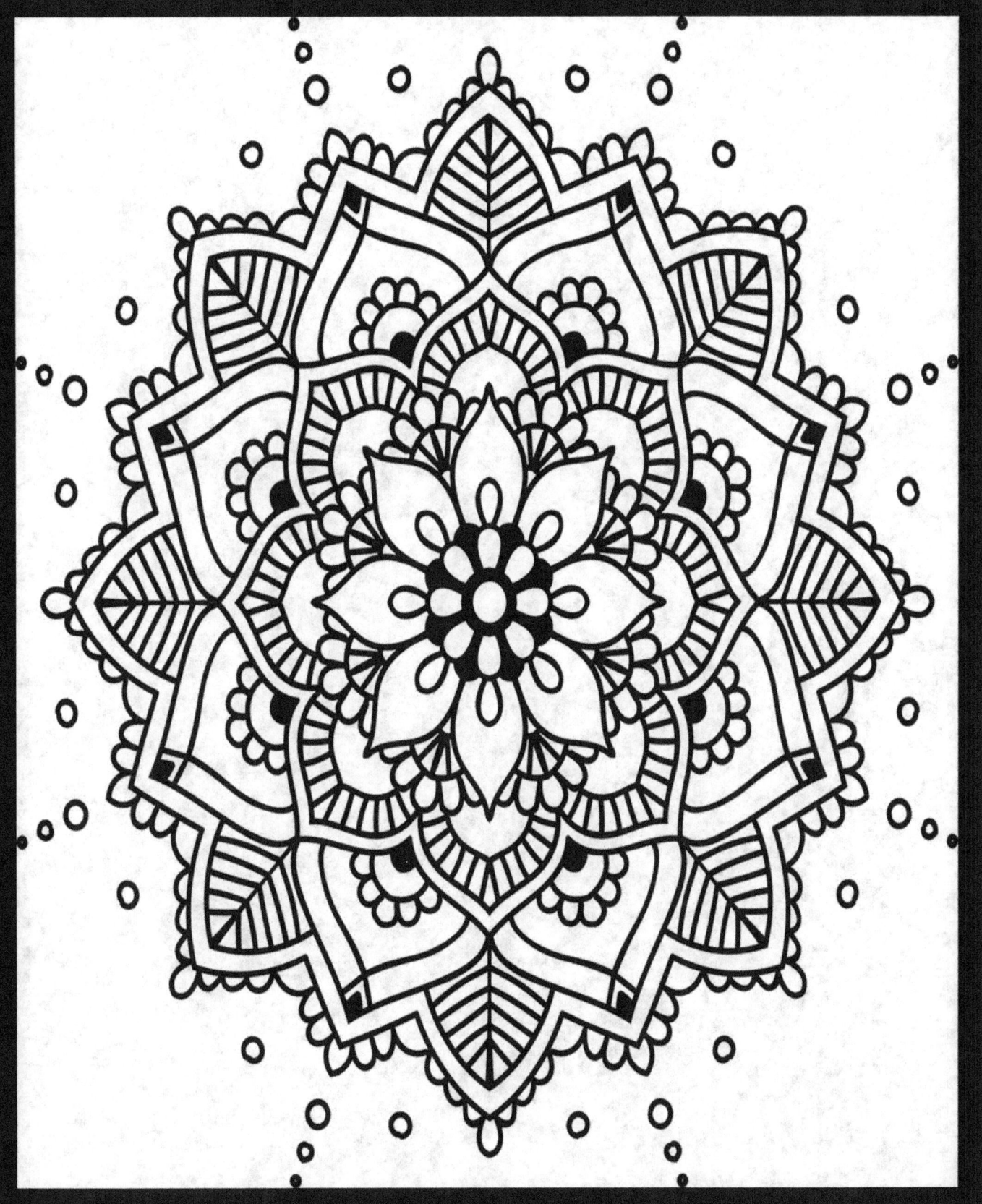

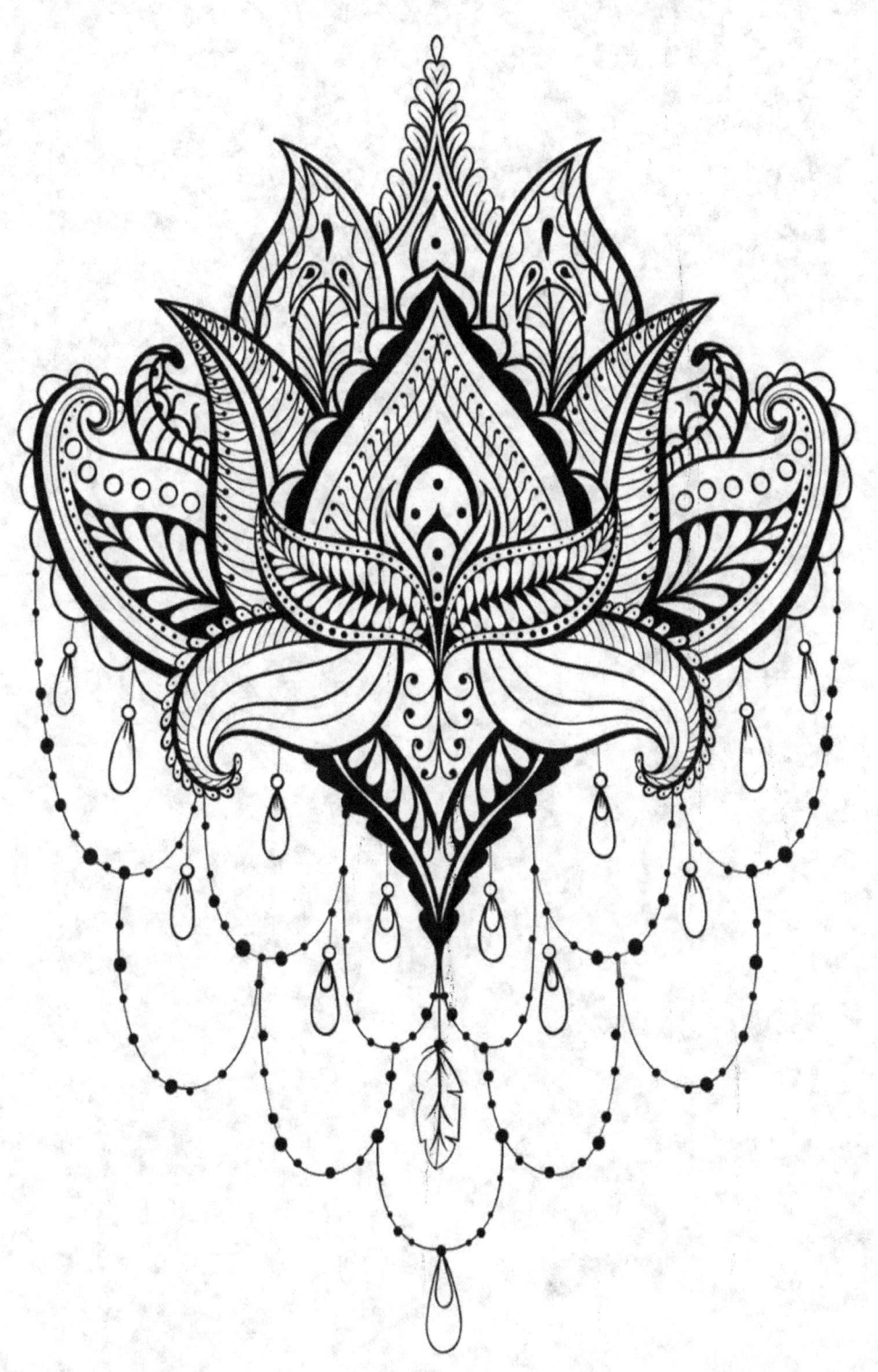

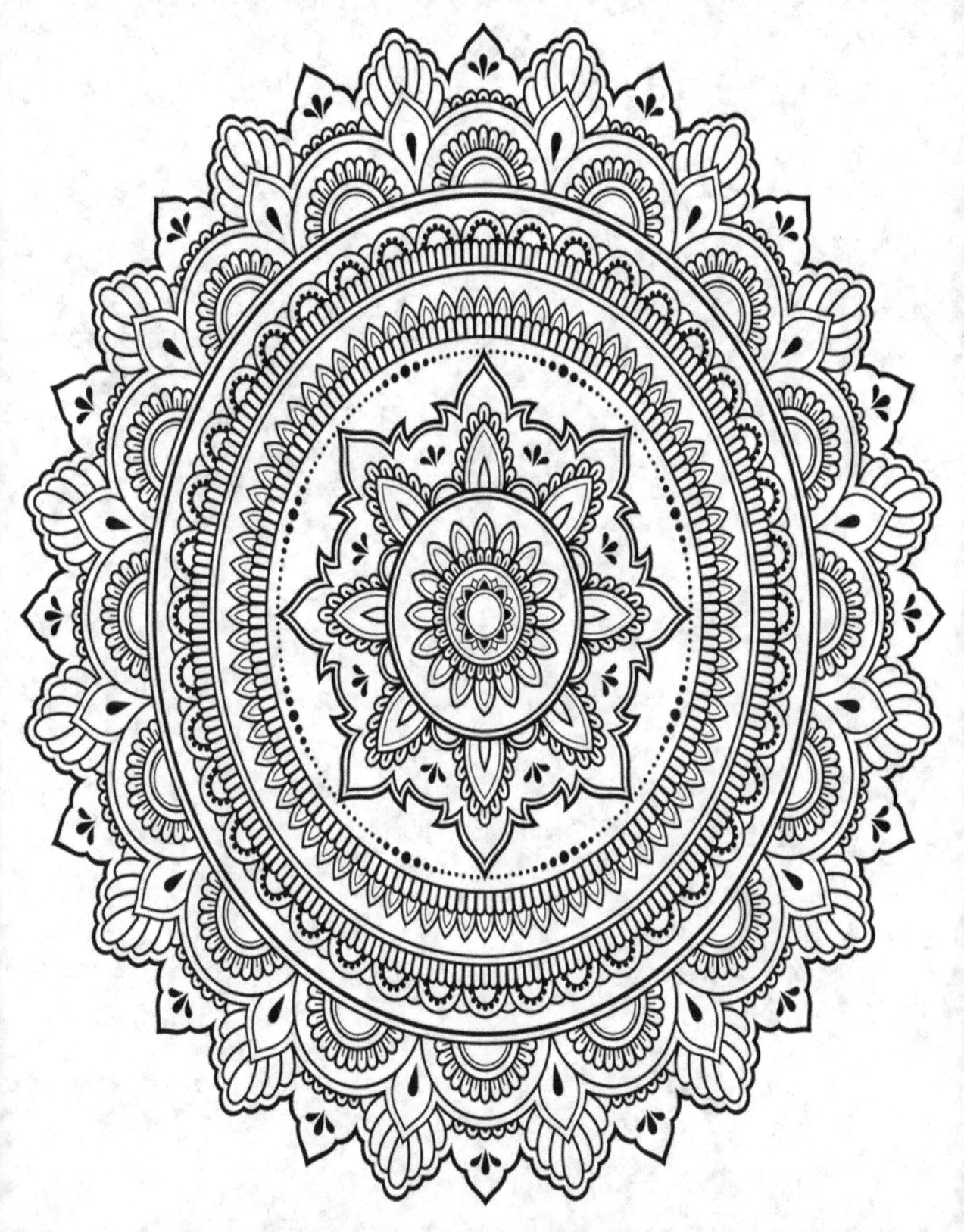

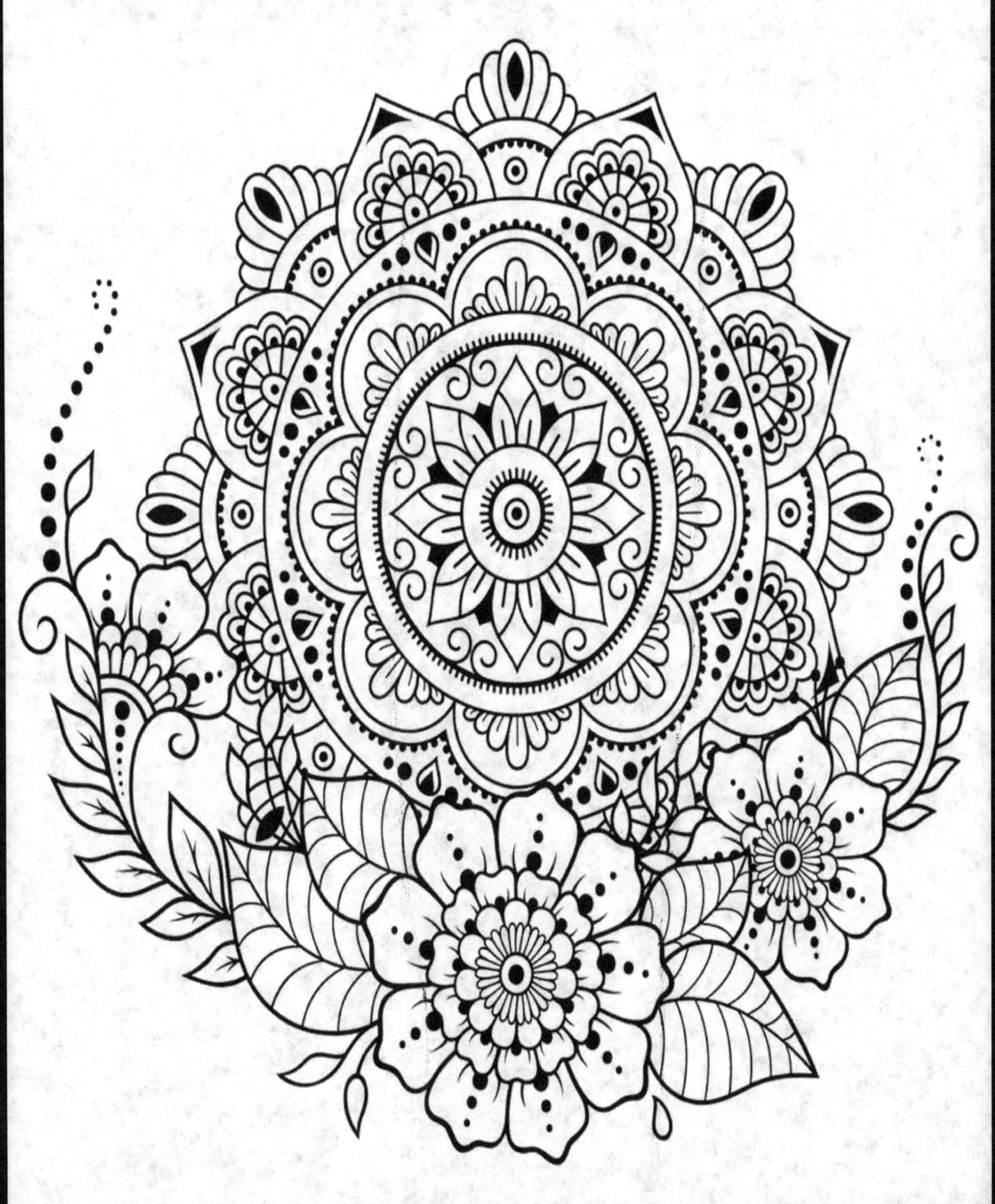

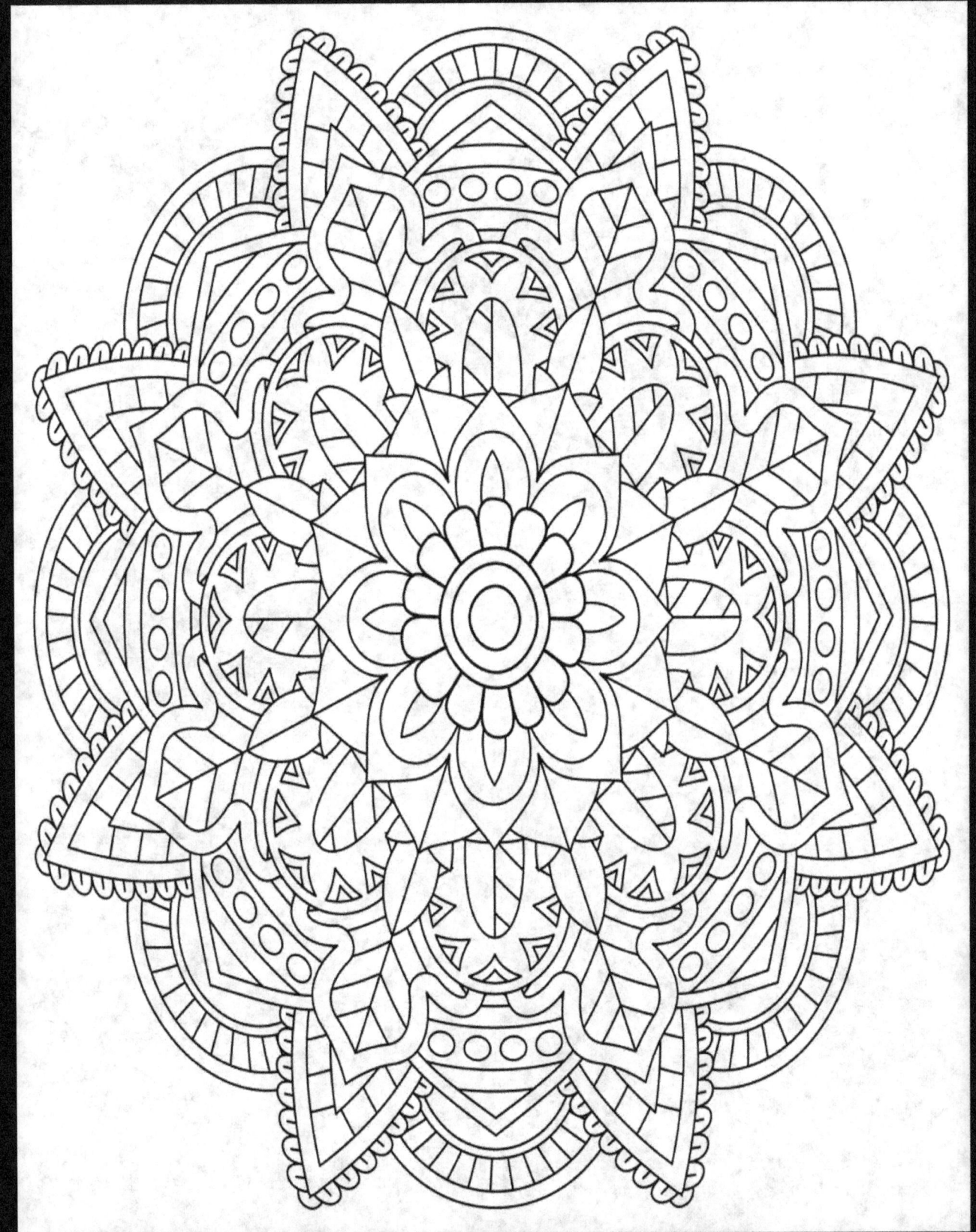

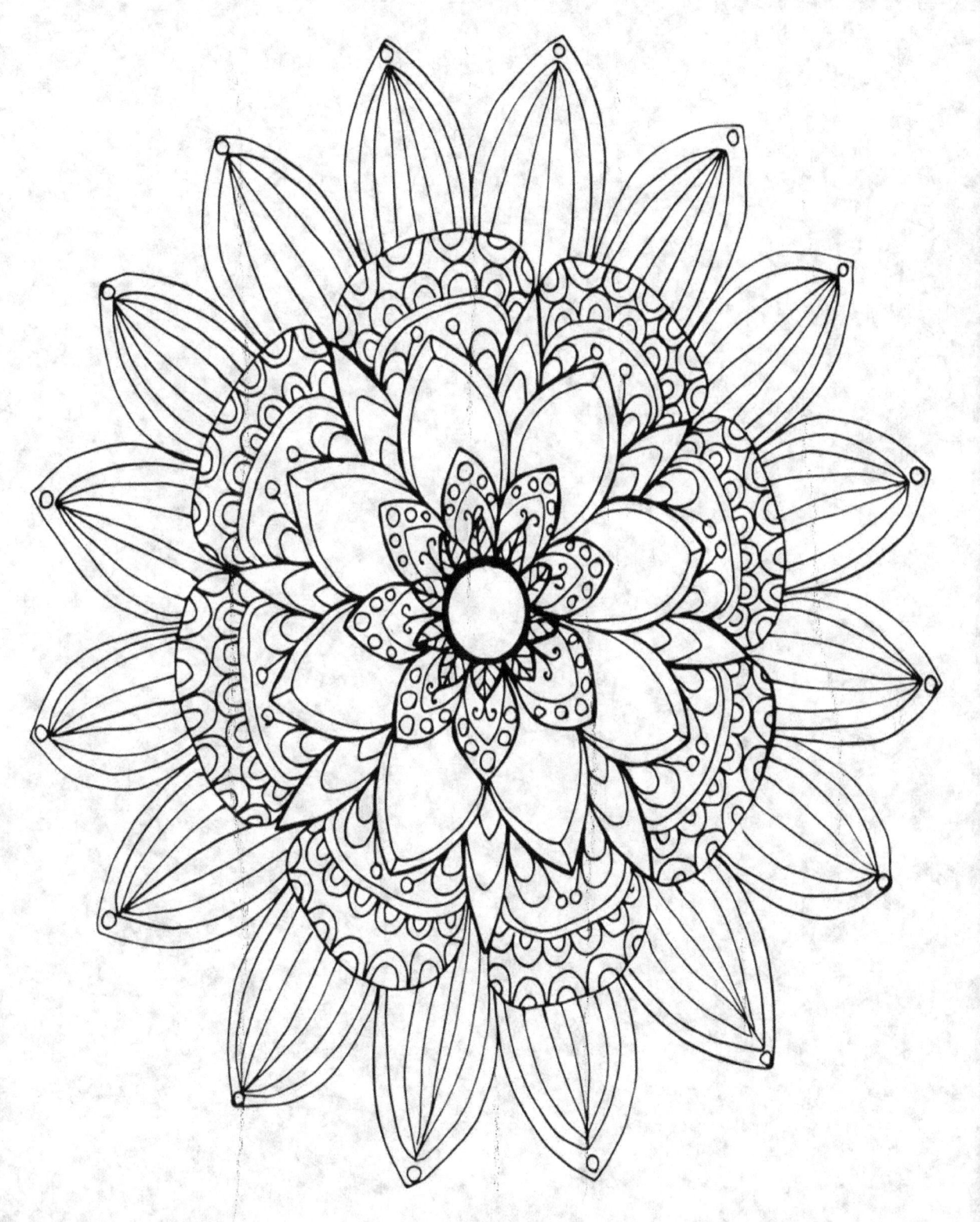

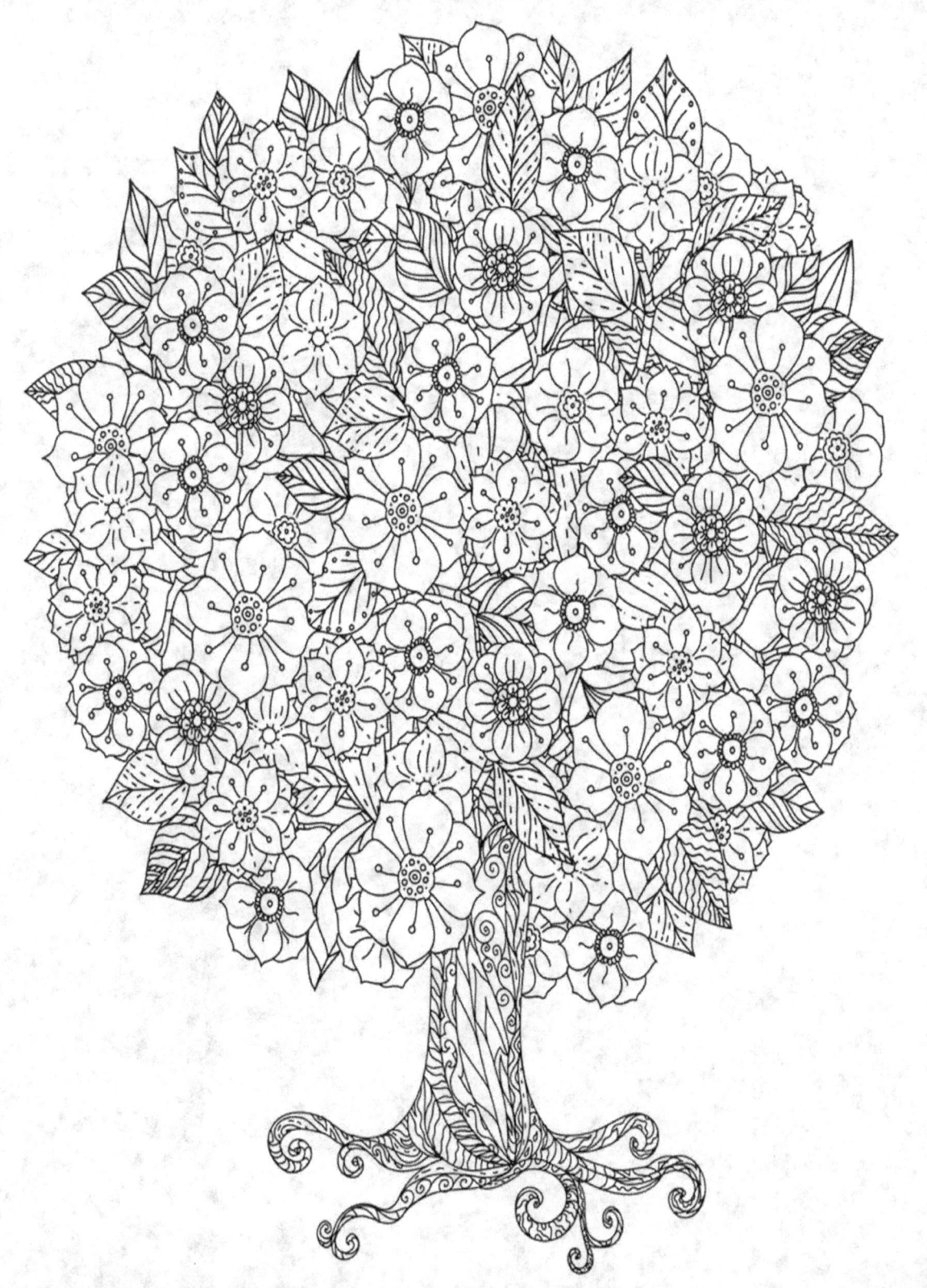

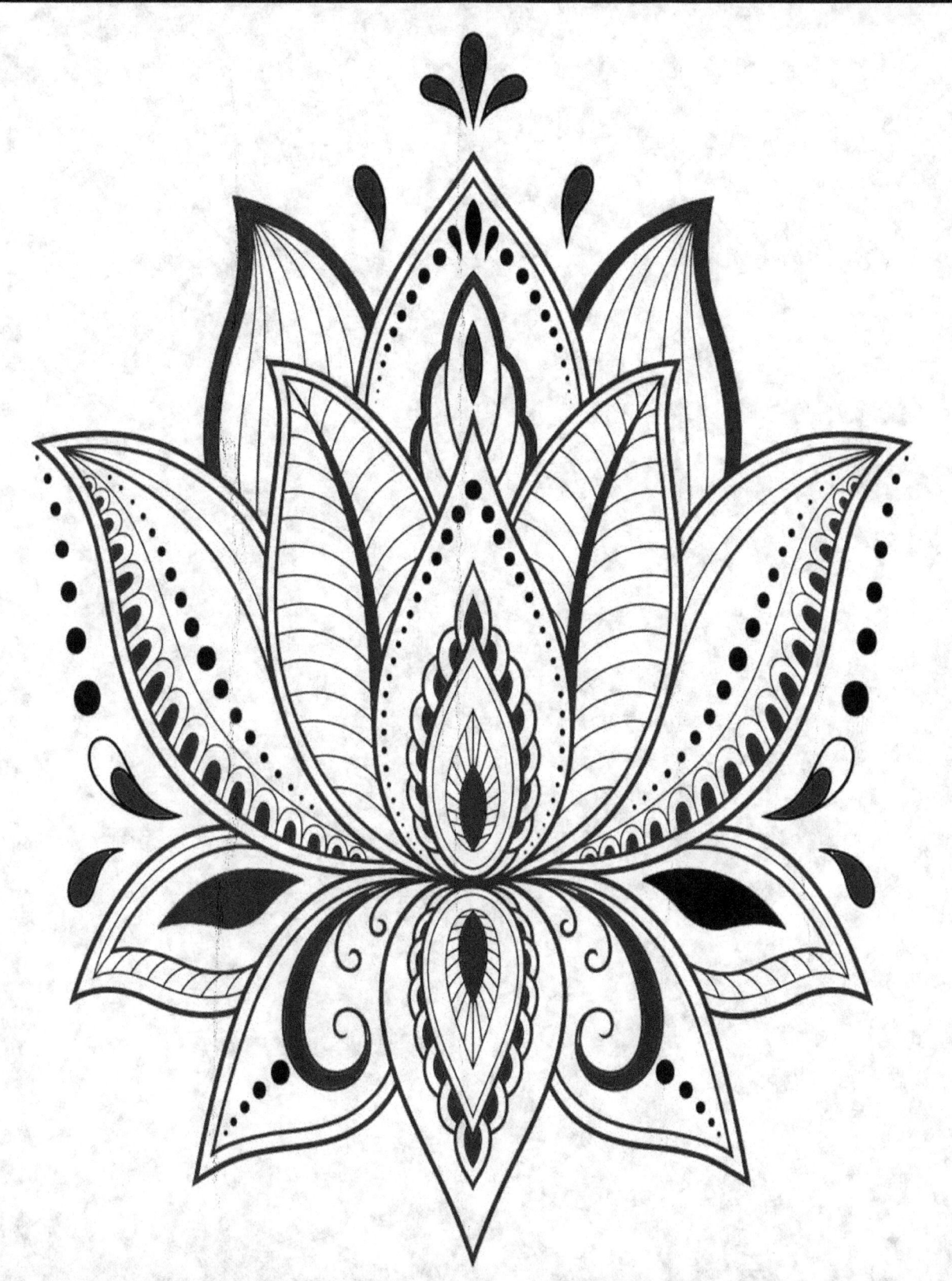

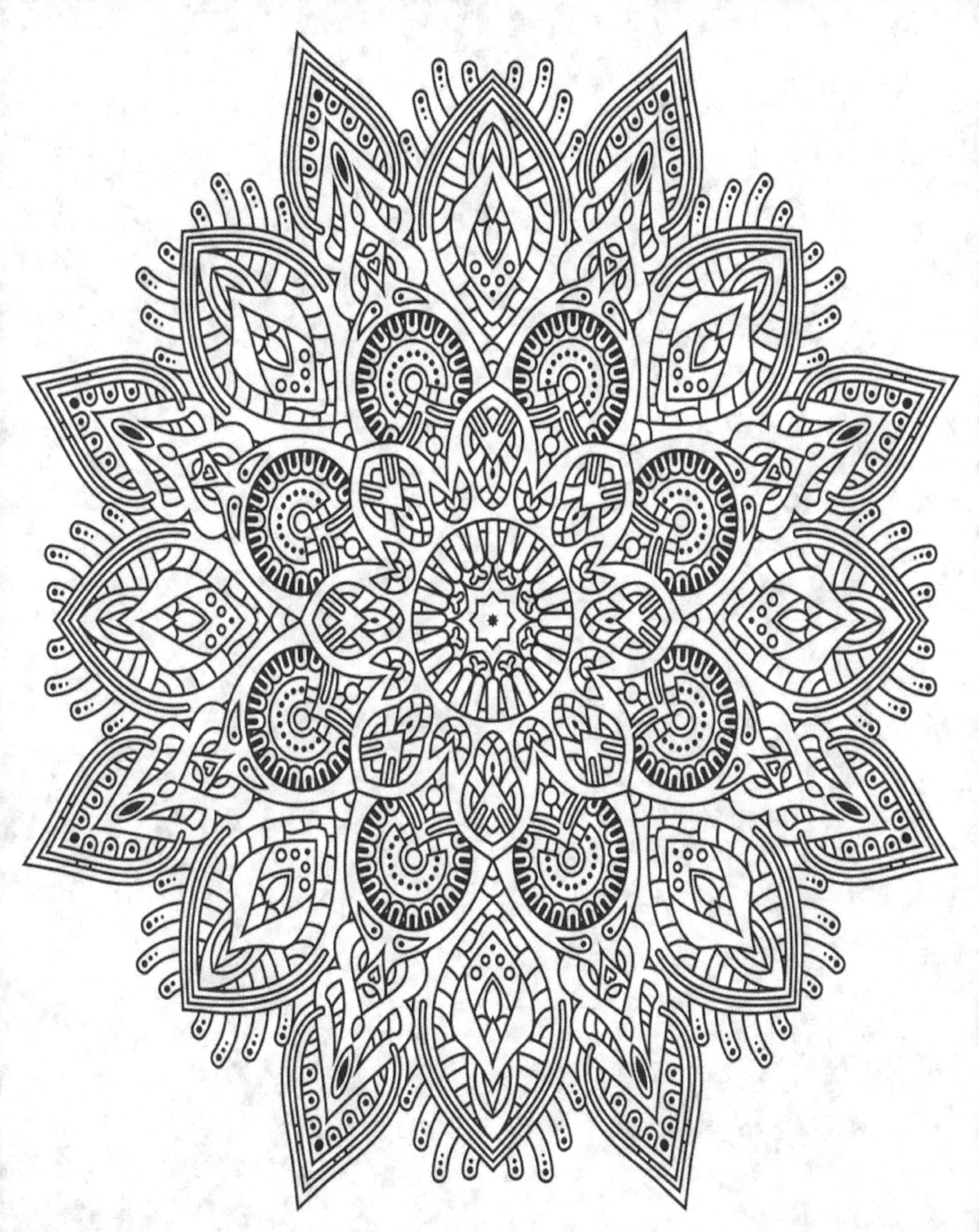

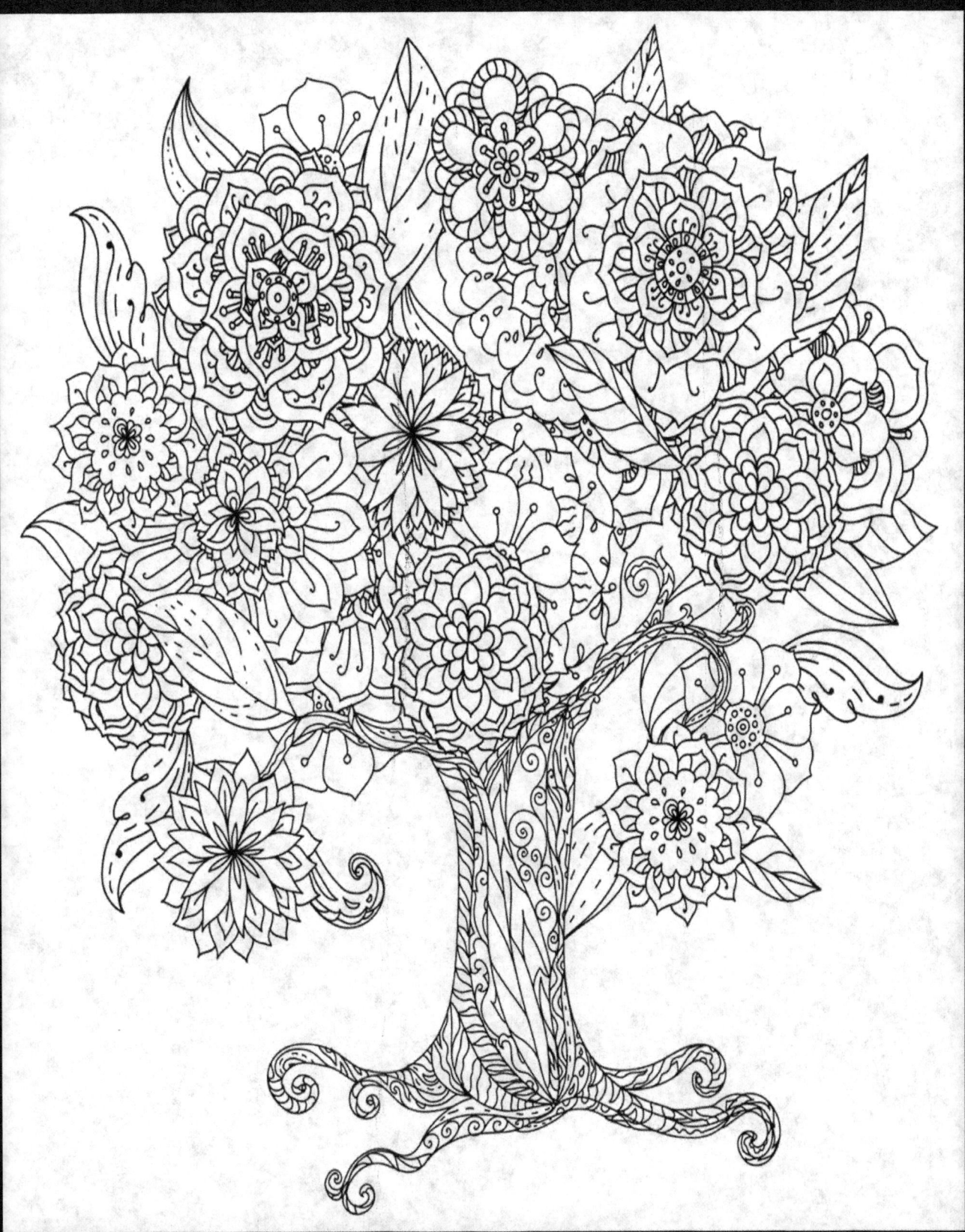

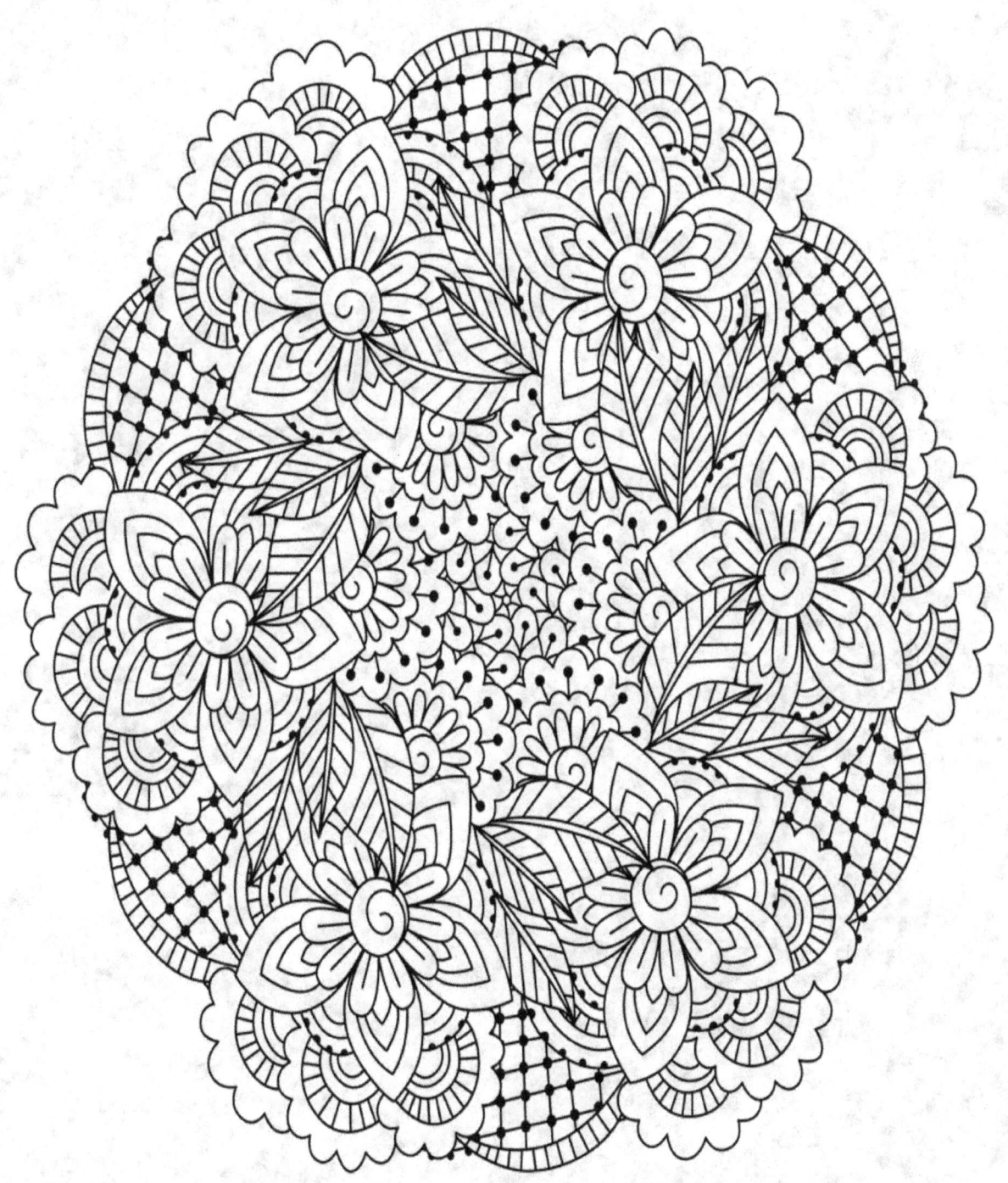

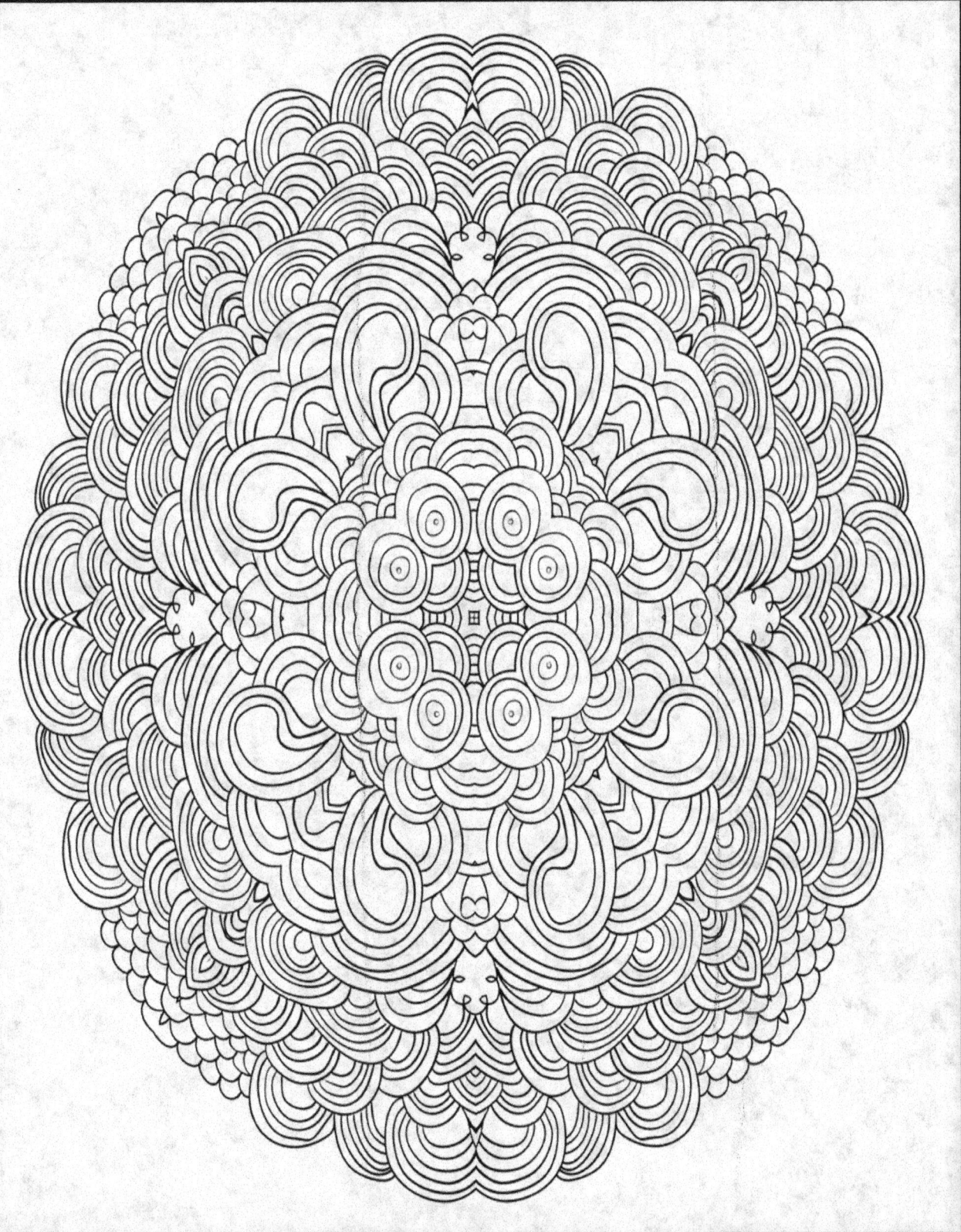

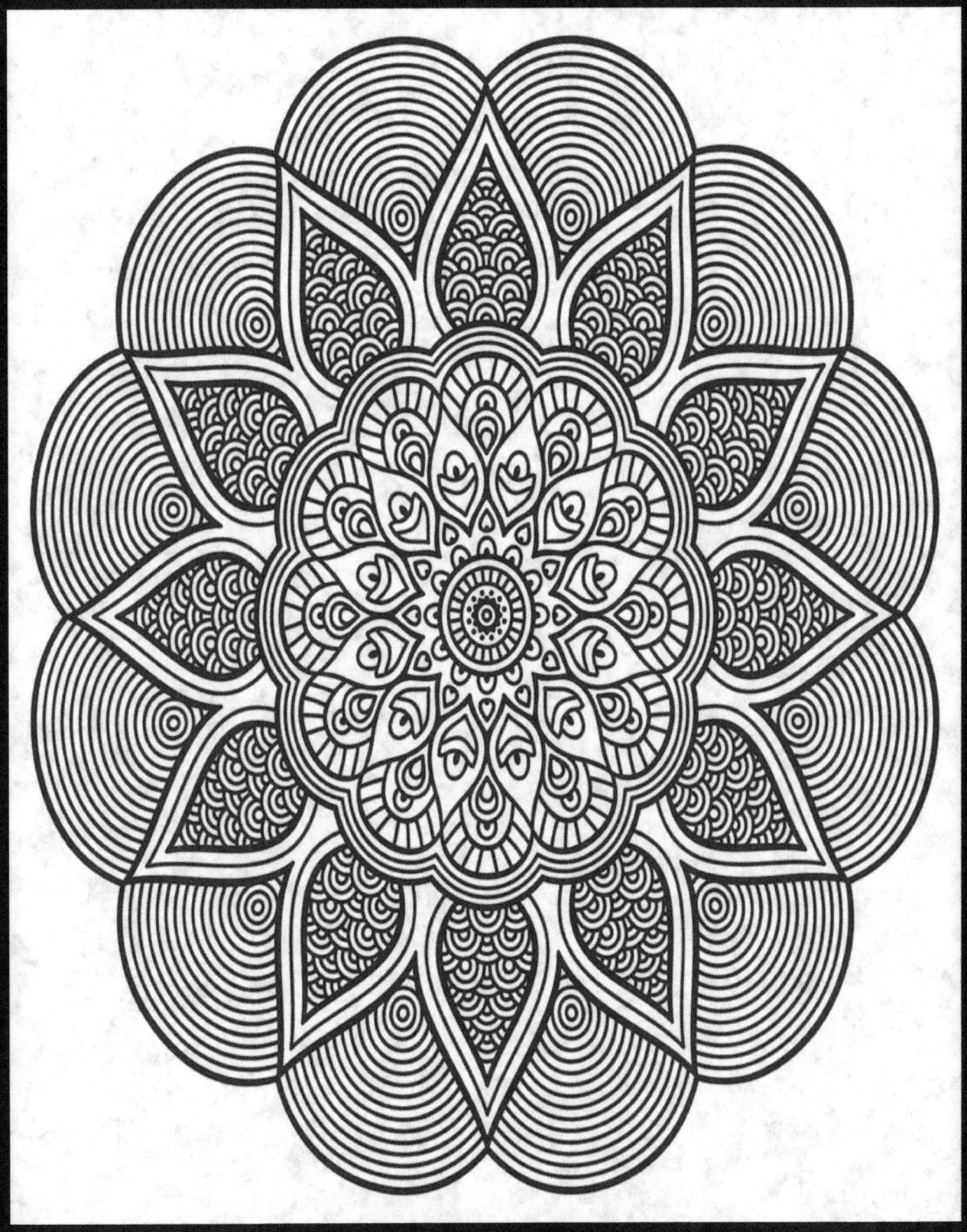

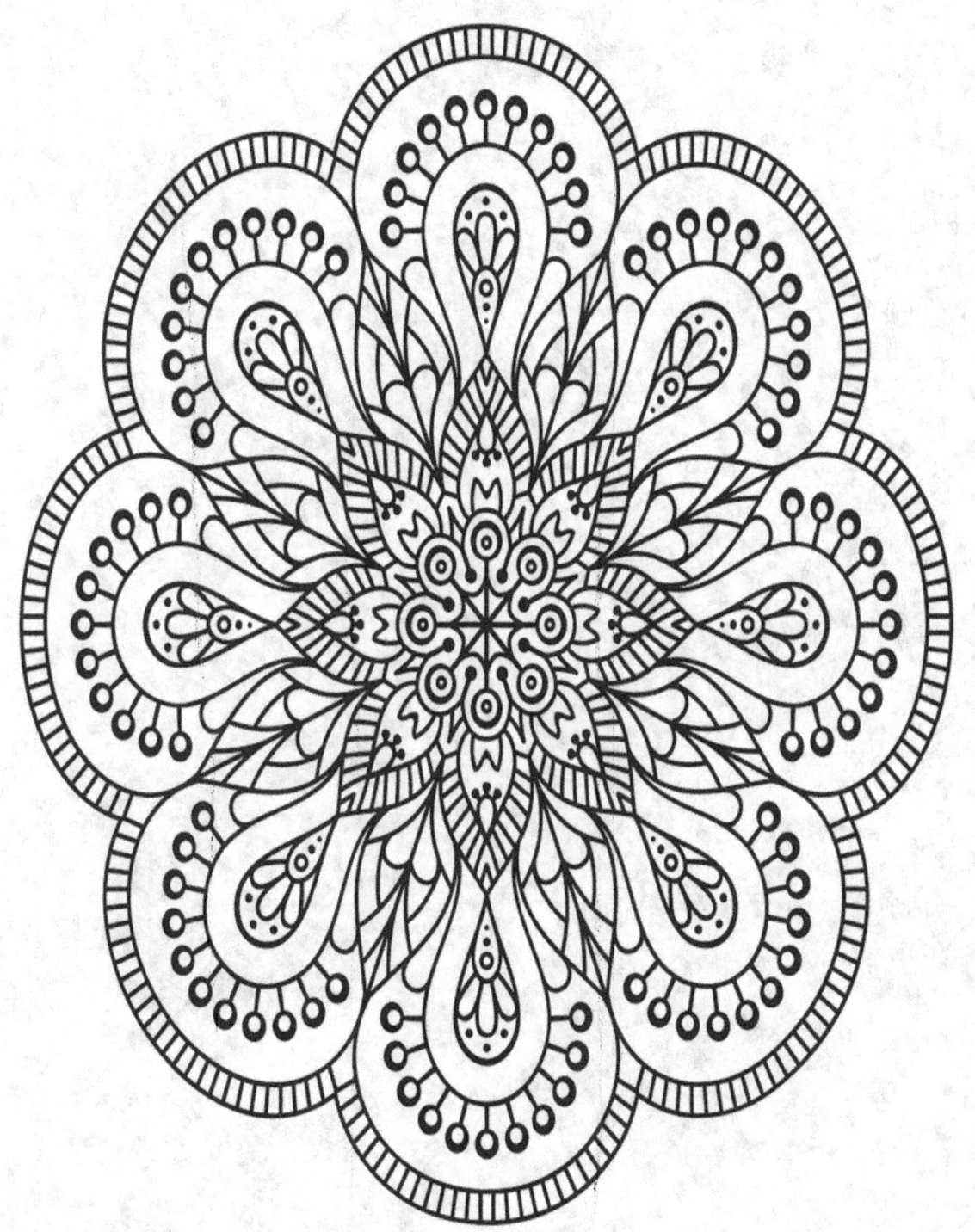

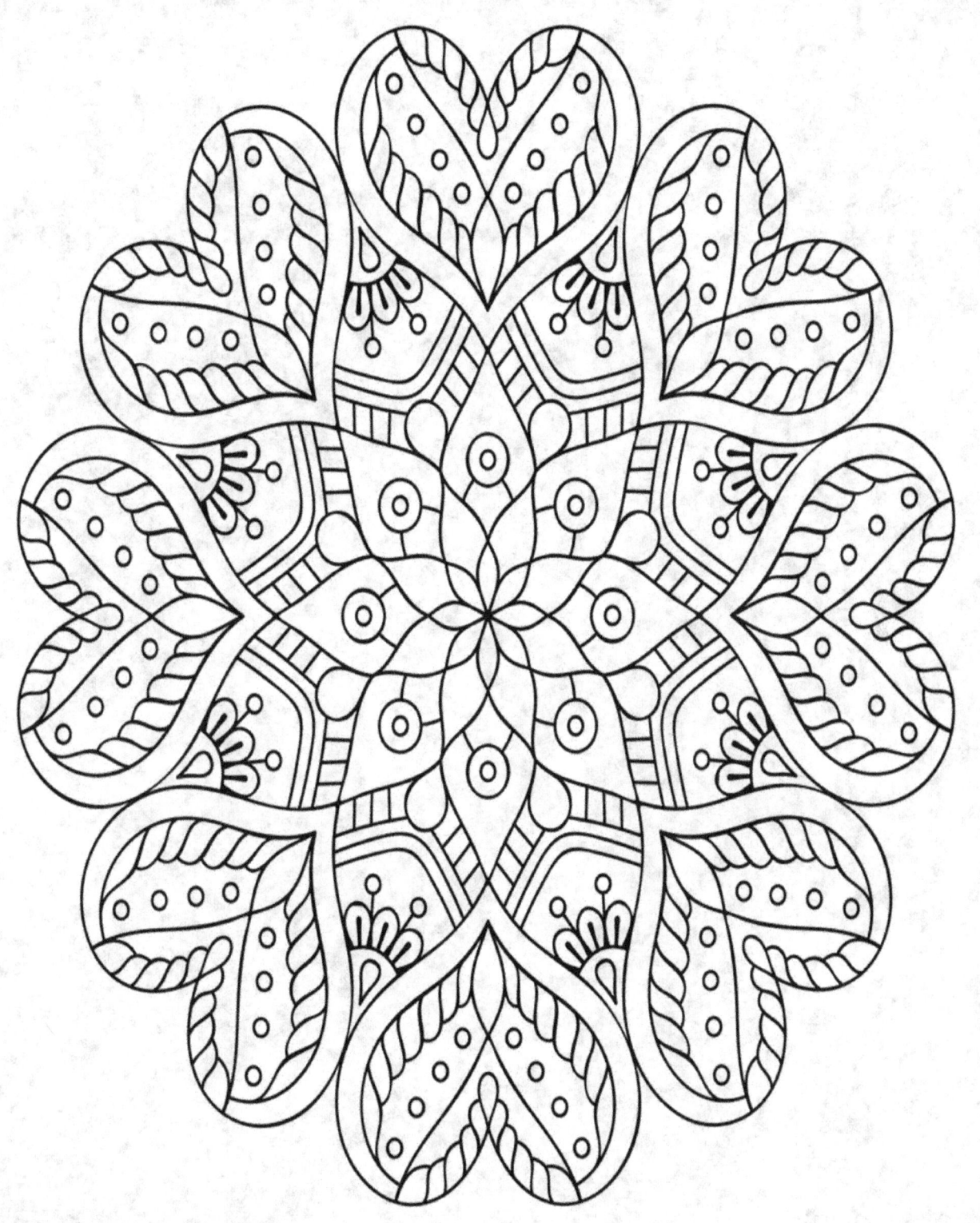

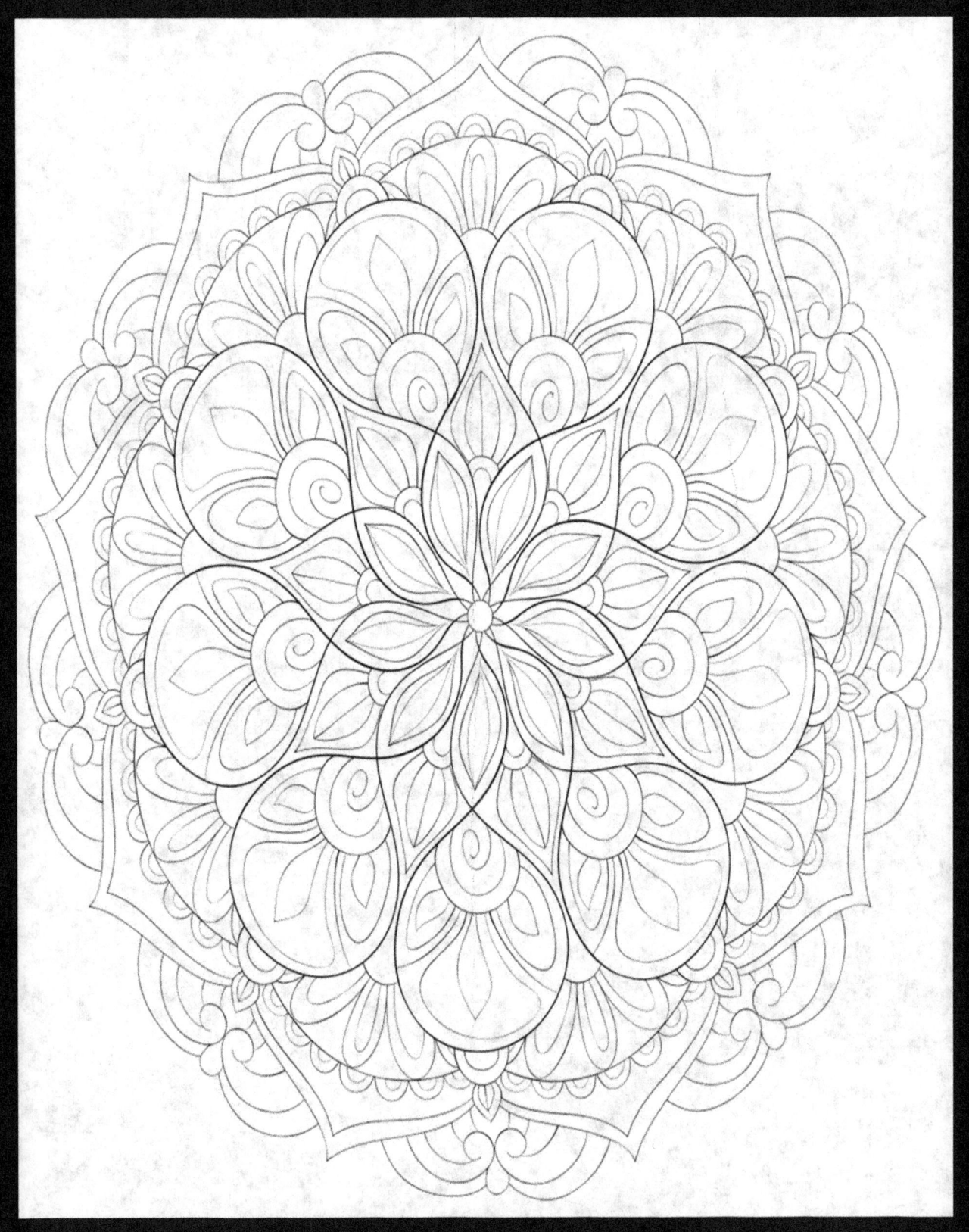

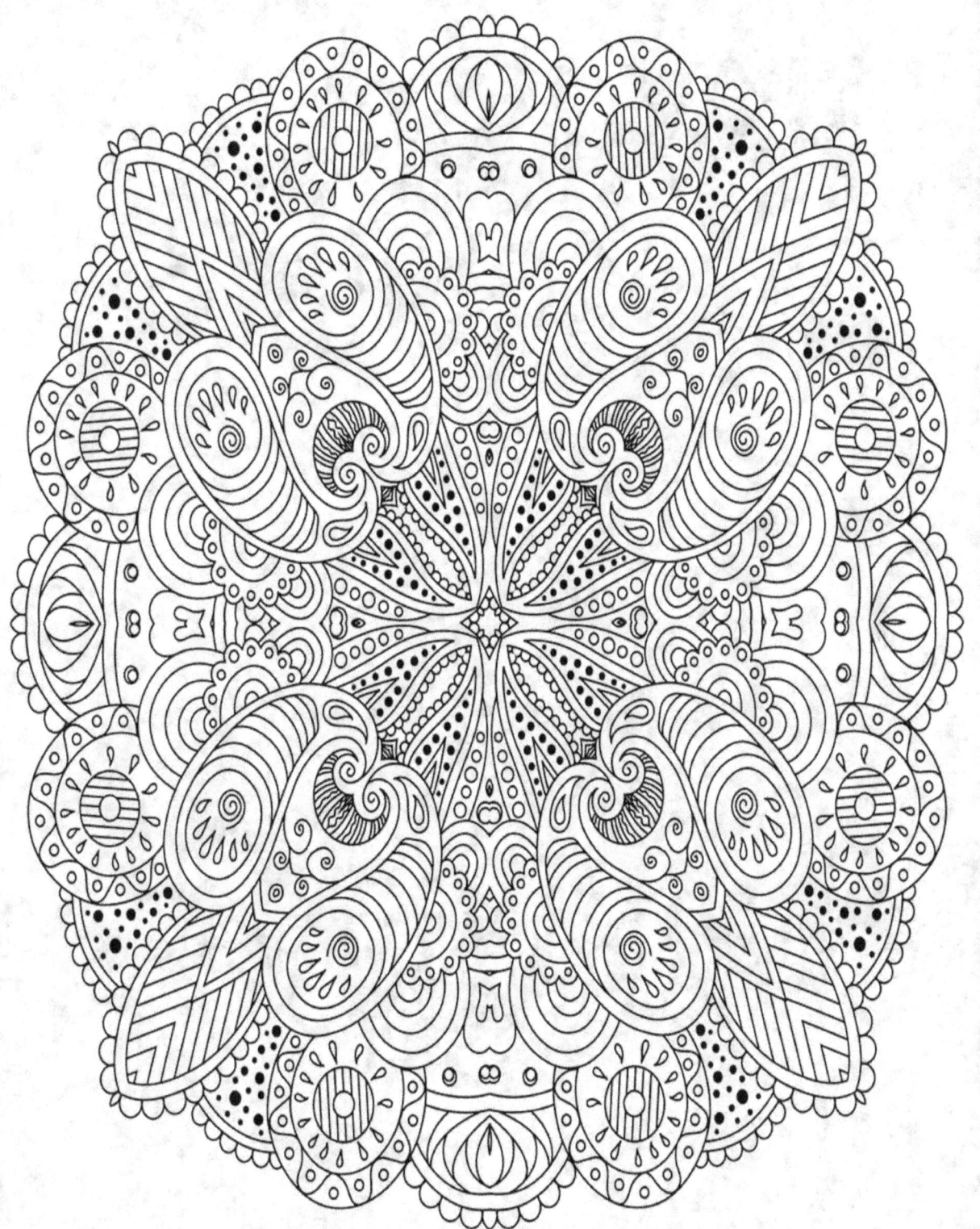

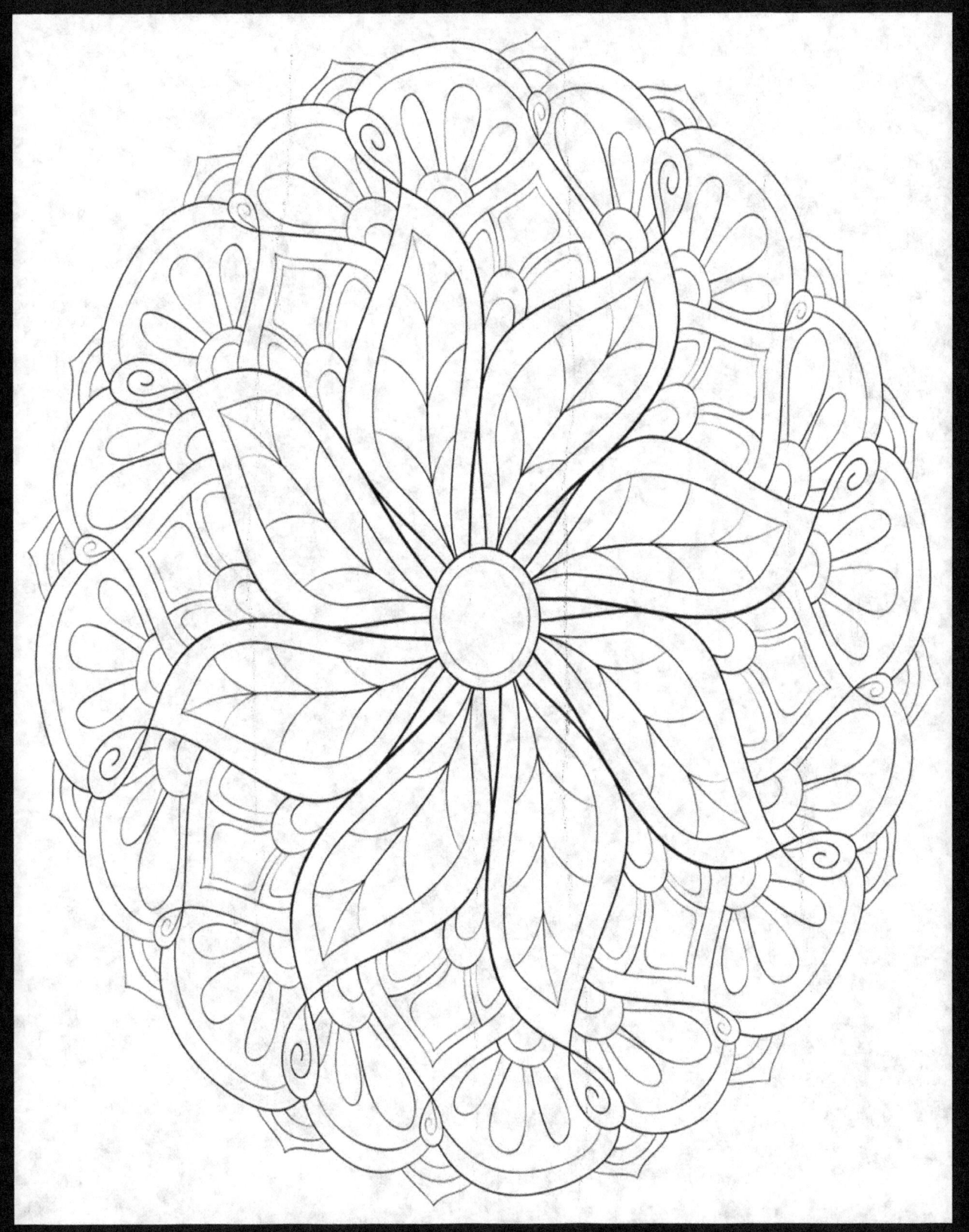

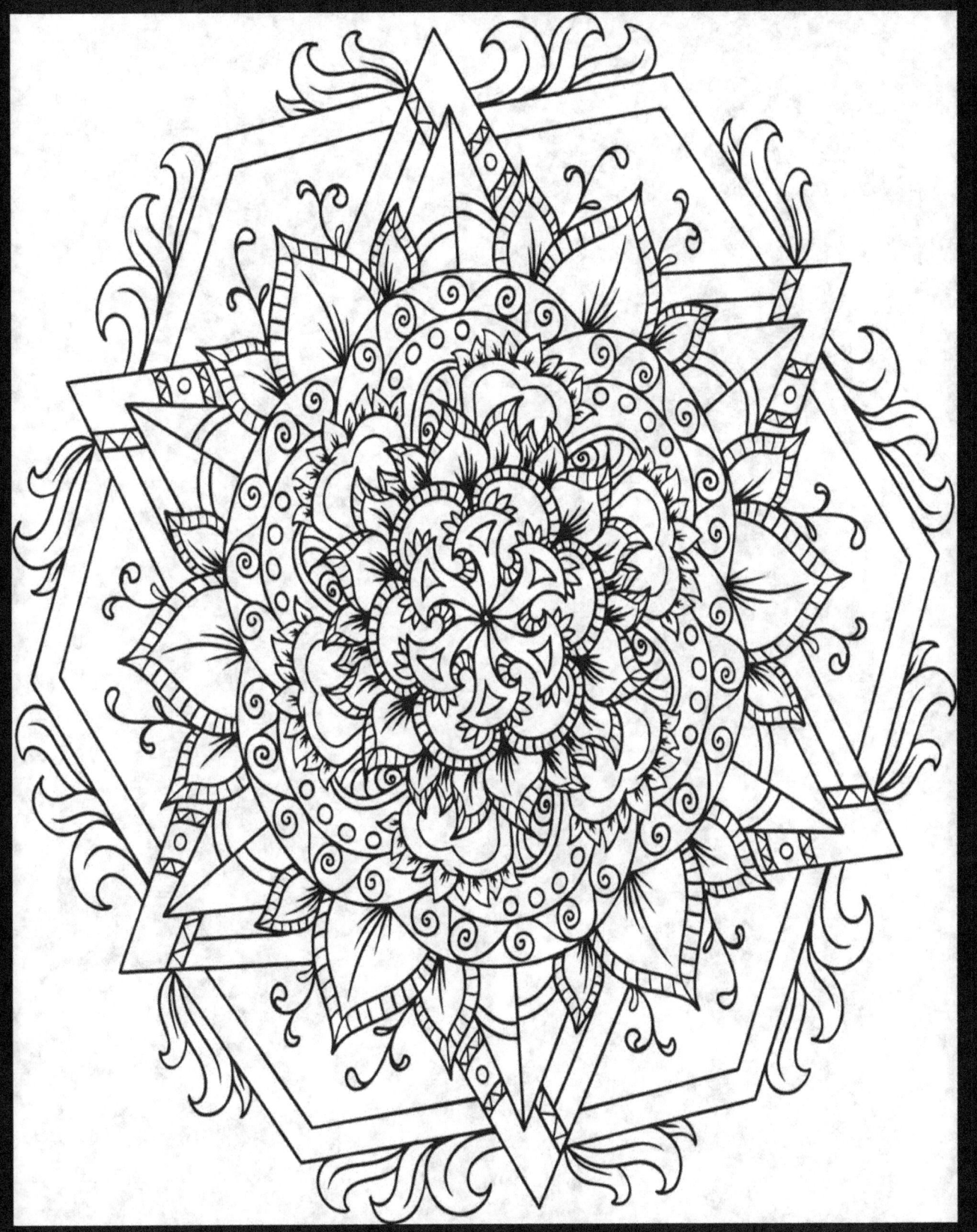

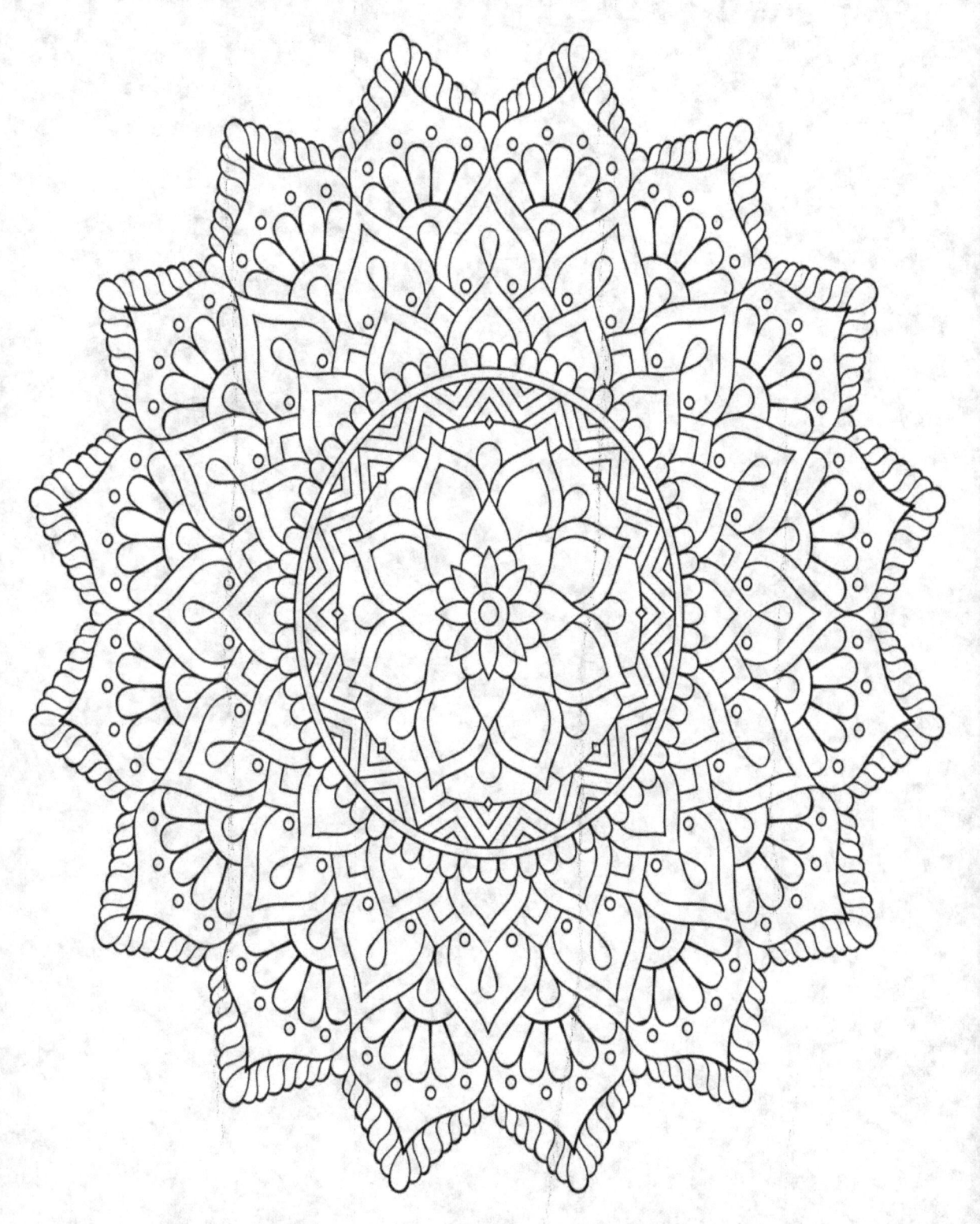

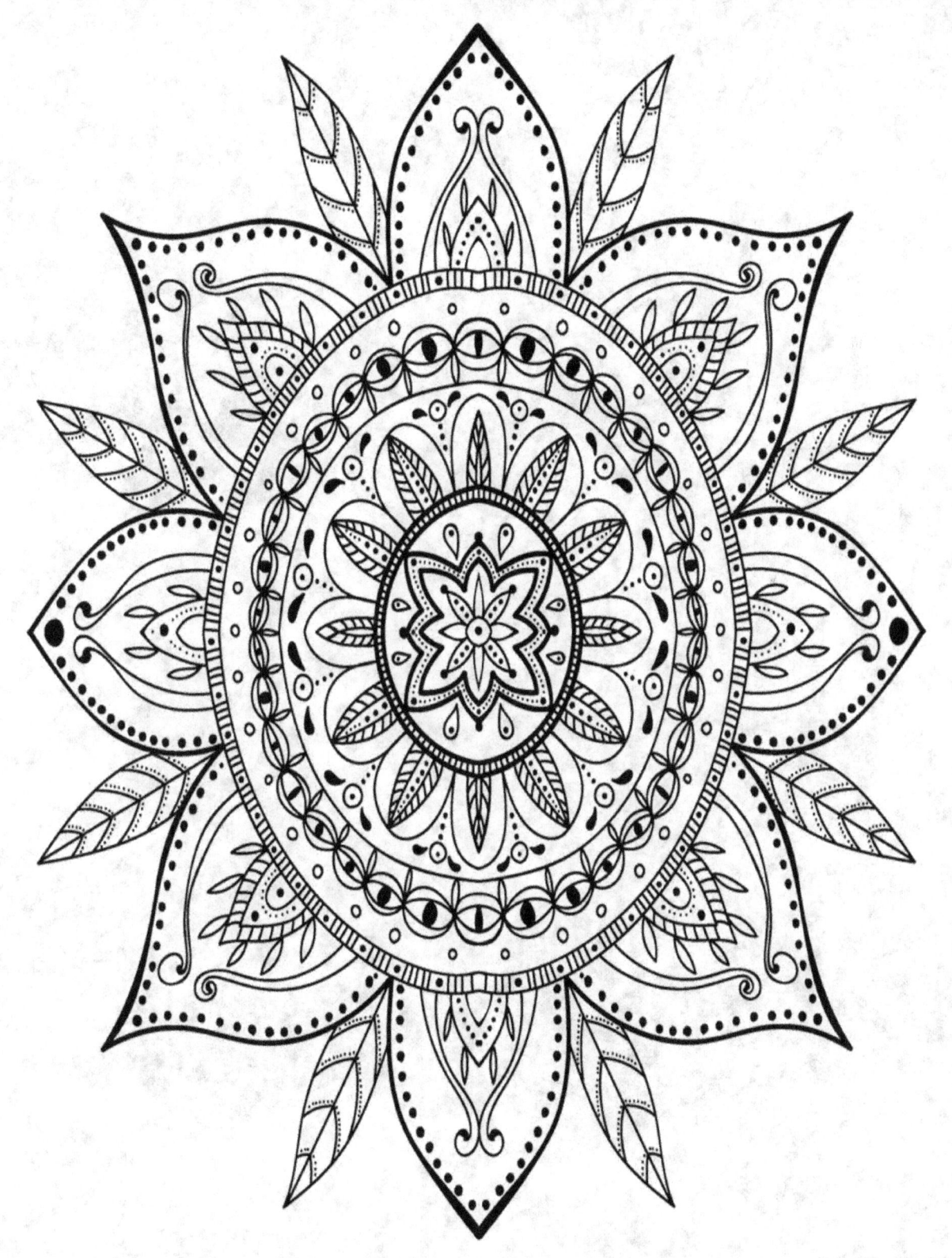

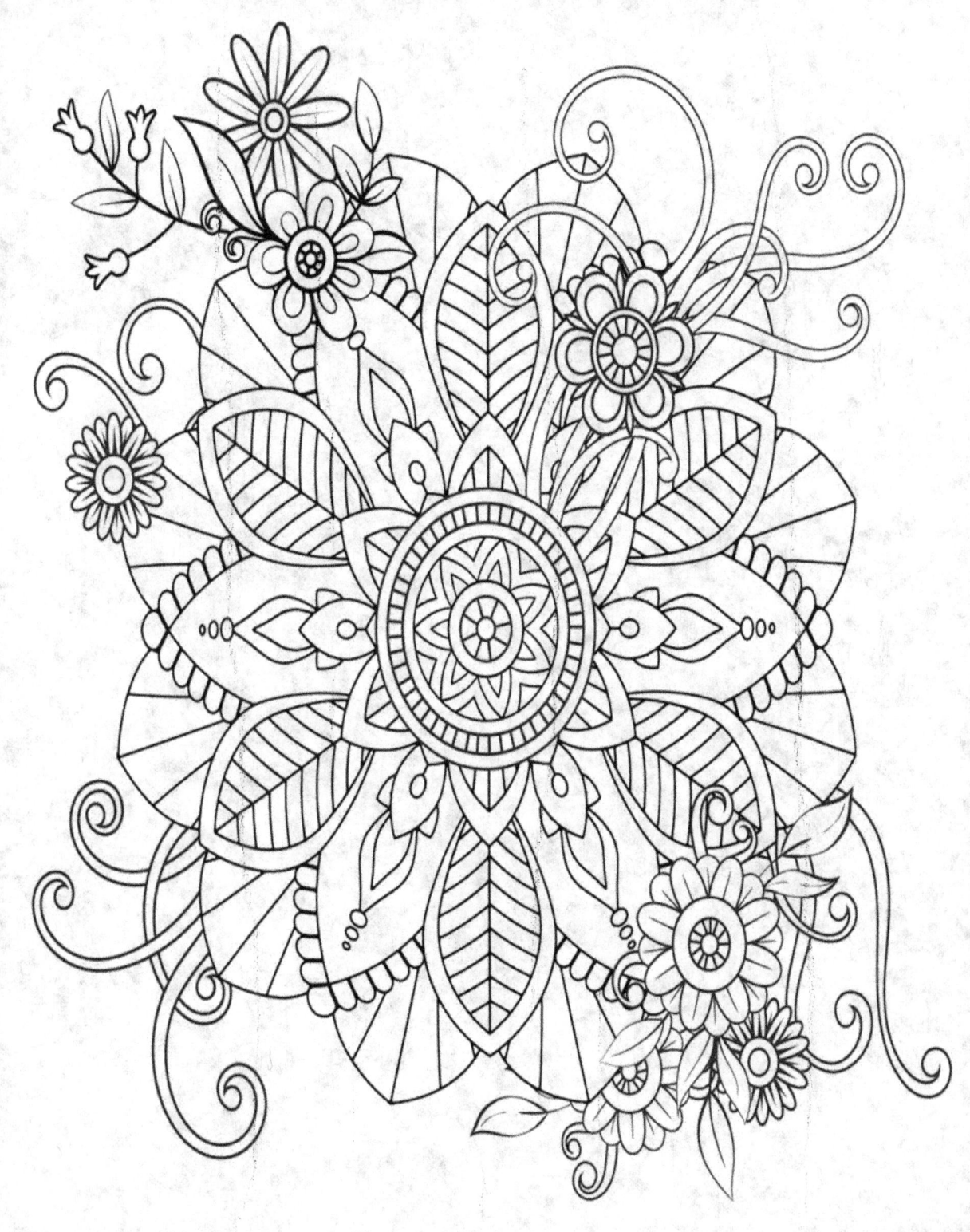

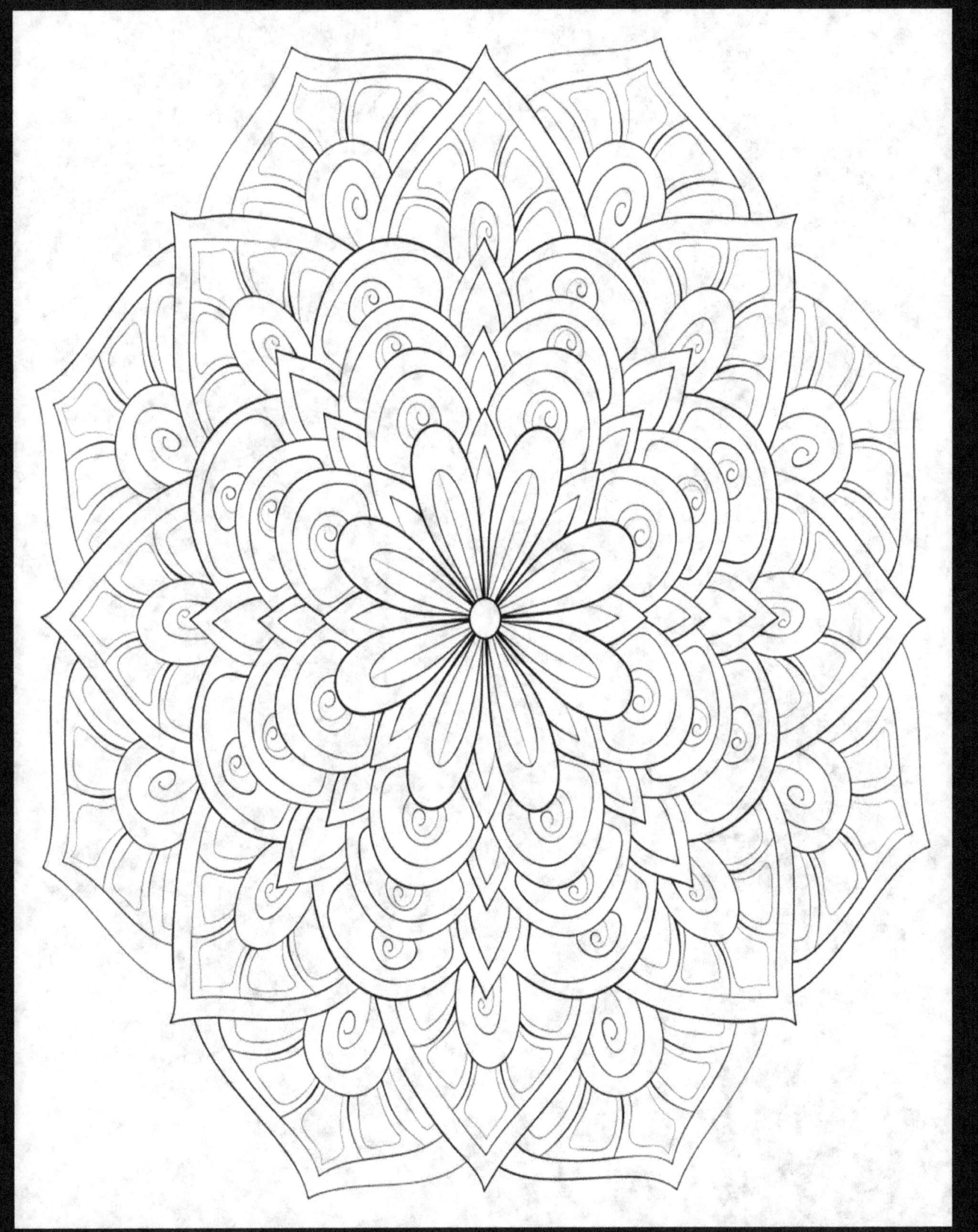

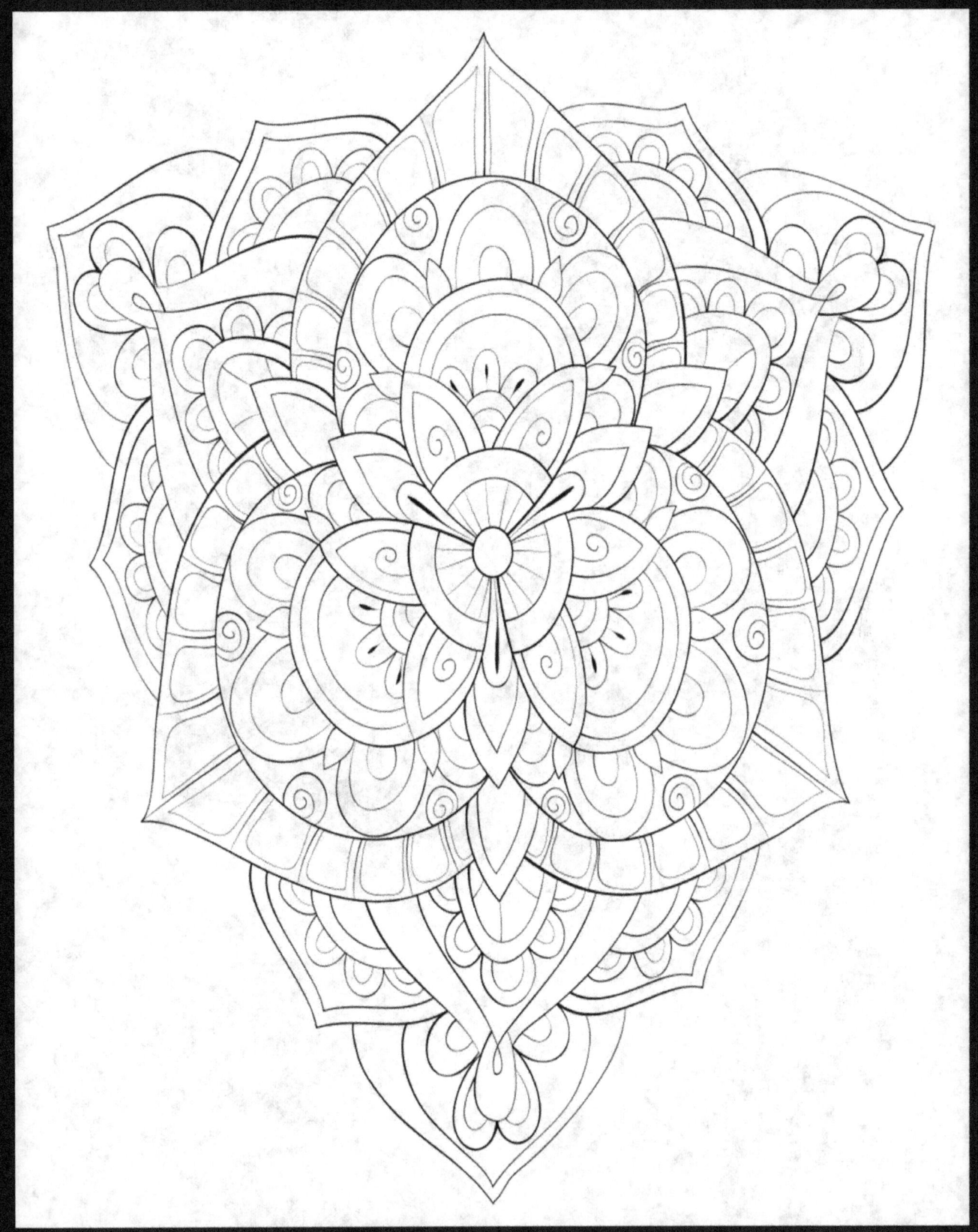

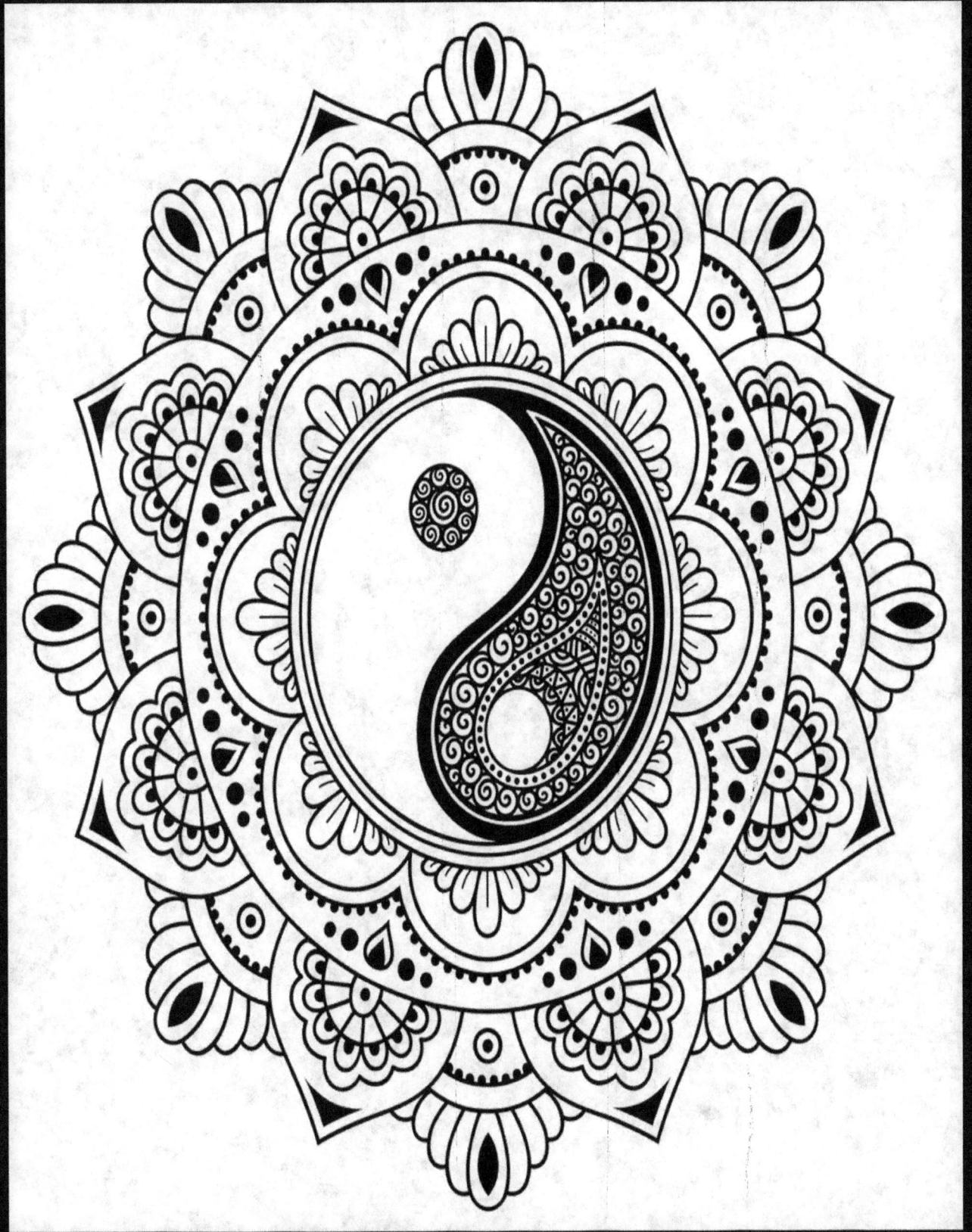

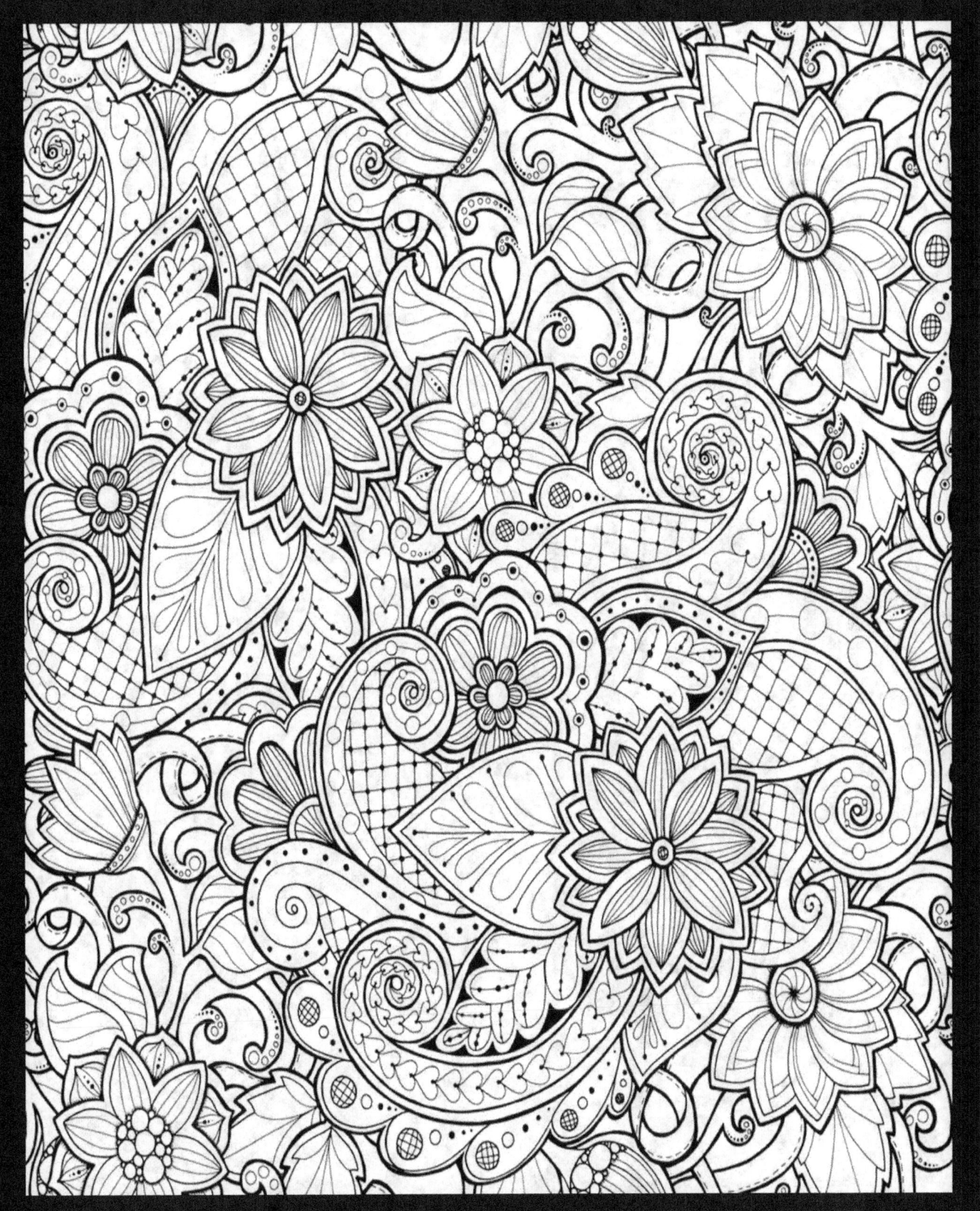

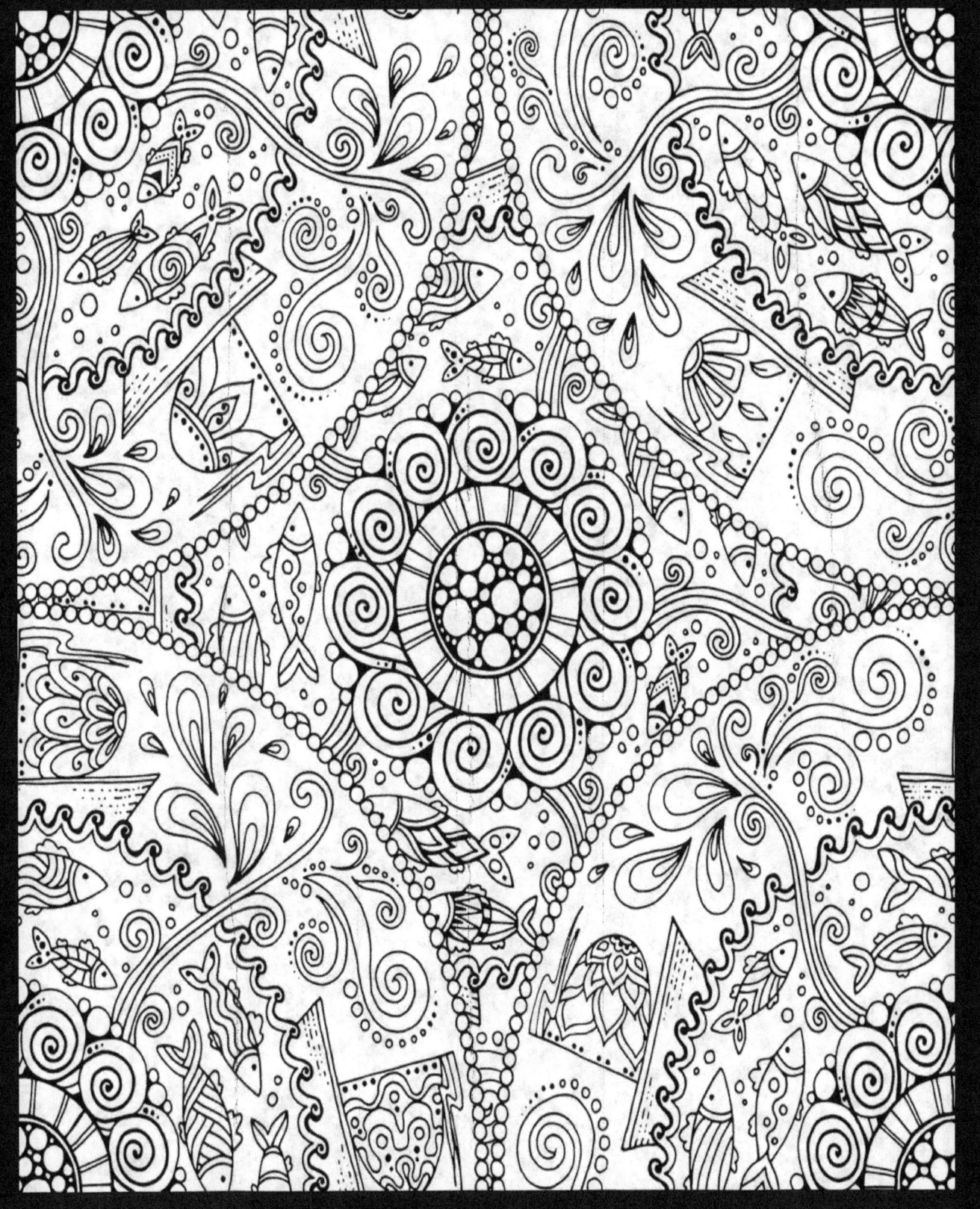

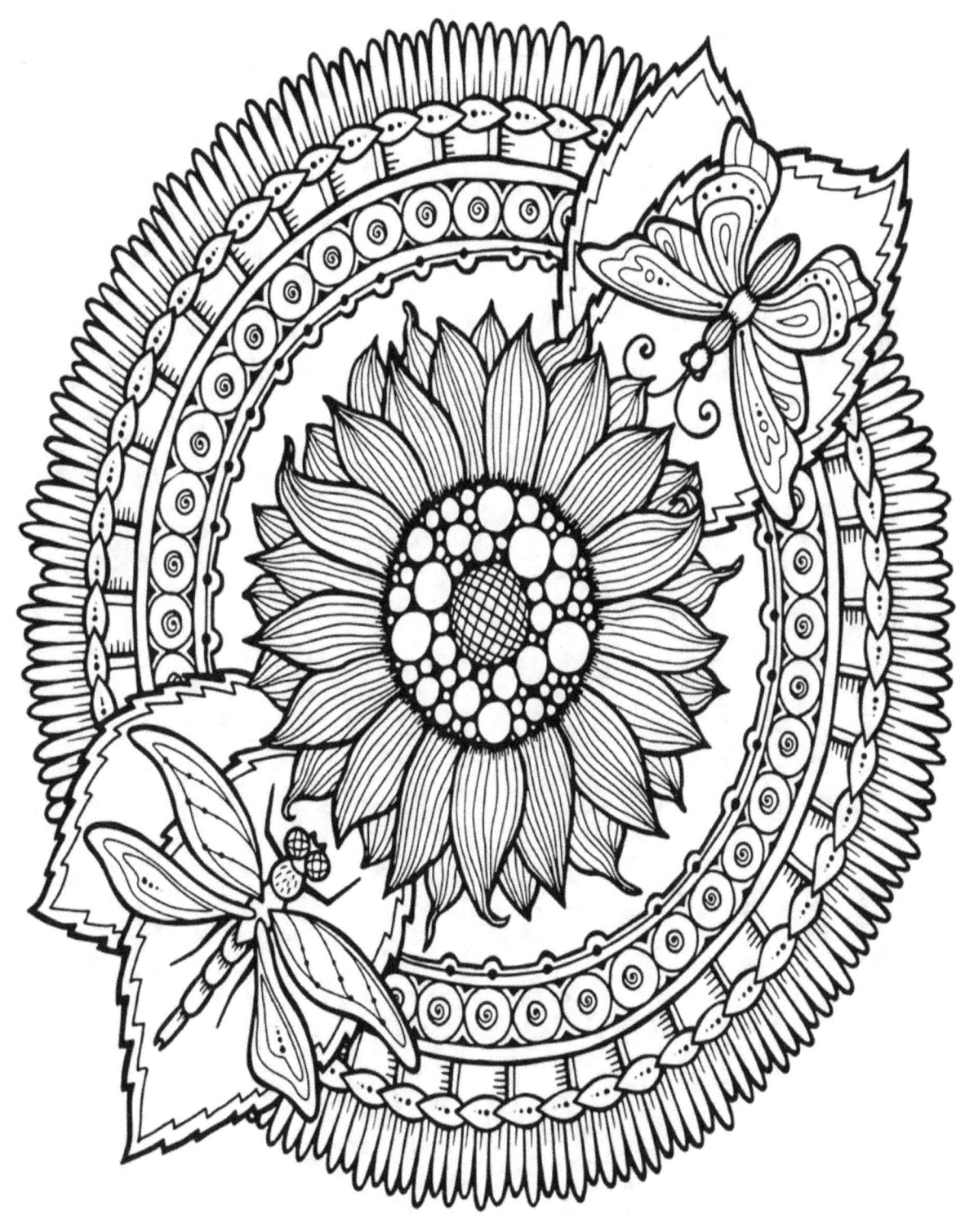

www.ingramcontent.com/pod-product-compliance
Lightning Source LLC
Chambersburg PA
CBHW080506220526
45465CB00006B/2393